What Are They Saying About John?

Gerard S. Sloyan

PAULIST PRESS
New York/Mahwah, N.J.

Library of Congress Cataloging-in-Publication Data

Sloyan, Gerard Stephen, 1919–
    What are they saying about John? / Gerard S. Sloyan.
        p.   cm.
    Includes bibliographical references.
    ISBN 0-8091-3238-9
    1. Bible. N.T. John—Criticism, interpretation, etc.   I. Title.
BS2615.2.S565   1991
226.5'06—dc20   91-11907
                                                          CIP

Published by Paulist Press
997 Macarthur Boulevard
Mahwah, New Jersey 07430

Printed and bound in the
United States of America

Contents

Introduction

Surely this is a foolhardy venture. Scholarly writing on the gospel according to John is well-nigh boundless. To attempt a report on the output of the last twenty years reduces its bulk somewhat, as does confining the work largely to that done in English. A service can undoubtedly be rendered by a report such as this to people who notice the appearance of books and articles but do not have the time to read them, or who remember the status of John studies the last time they did them but have been too busy at other matters to engage in an update. A third class of readers is made up of those who know the text of John but are unfamiliar with the wars that have raged over its purpose, time and place of origin, mode of composition, rhetorical character, and so on. Given the broad range of persons who may consult these pages, the best writing style seemed to be a clear expository one with a minimum of technical terms and transliterated Greek. When terms of scholarly shorthand occur (like "eschatology"), which it would be tedious to many to define, the readers who find them new are referred to an unabridged dictionary.

The scope of writings on John, chosen arbitrarily, is the years 1970–90. A chapter introductory to this period is placed first. One way of proceeding would have been to group books and articles according to subject matter, theme, or general tendency. This requires a gift of synthesis the present writer may not possess. There was another inhibiting factor at work. The technique runs the risk of betraying the scholars thus classified. After writing 380-page books filled with nuance, they can find themselves lumped to-

1

gether in a parentheses that says ("so, too, Carpenter, Falegname, and Zimmermann").

The route chosen in the pages that follow may be even more freighted with peril. It tries to convey the essence of long and complex arguments by transmitting sizable segments of them. Even here the digester may make serious errors in catching the main thrust of a book (less likely, an article). Any scholarly author may cry "Inadequate grasp!" but my hope is that none cries "Foul!" Judgment on the quality of the writings reported on is largely left to the reader, a clear possibility if enough evidence has been presented. The subject-matter index thus becomes the key to using this book. As to works not reported on, consulting the multiple citations in the works here mentioned can remedy that.

My one regret is that the list of solid *religious* writings based on the gospel according to John is so brief. Popularizations of scholarship abound,[1] but the dependable writing on this gospel suitable for contemplation and prayer, public or private, is regrettably small. Perhaps the exegetical labor had to be done first.

1
The Landmark Commentaries

What Are They Saying About John? They are saying any number of things: some wise, some profound; some historical, some theological; some homiletical, some *religionsgeschichtlich*, a genre which at times is neither historical nor religious. And, yes, some are saying religious things about the fourth gospel (which is its sequence in most manuscript codices and all modern Bibles). That there is religious writing on John is as it should be, for its final compiler, along with any who may have produced parts of it, thought their product a religious book. Its purpose—indeed its only purpose—was that the hearer of Jesus' signs recorded in this book should have life by it through faith that Jesus is the Christ, the Son of God. Such was the author's declared intent as chapter 20 came to an end (vv. 30–31). The church included John in its canon for no other purpose. It is a book that promises life.

The First Hundred Years—Heracleon to Origen

There should be no need to review the difficulties experienced by "Jn"—as the canonical gospel shall be designated here, sometimes "FG" for the fourth gospel, and its final editor "John" without prejudging its authorship—in gaining acceptance much before 175. The interpretation given to it by gnostics who found it supportive of their position was influential. The anonymous late second-century Muratorian Canon, a fragment of 85 lines in bad Latin probably written at Rome, says in lines 9–16 that John wrote at the urging of his fellow disciples and bishops. They were to "tell one another whatever shall be revealed to each of us."[1] To Andrew, one of John's disciples, it was revealed that "John should write down everything in his own name, while all of them should review it." It was thus conceived of as a synthesis of the revelation shared with the twelve, coming last of the gospels. (The first line of the fragment, however, begins with mention not of Matthew but of Mark, then Luke.) The 1740 discovery of Lodovico Muratori explicitly rejects several writings as heretical. This may mean that its acceptance of John is an implicit response to certain heretics of Asia Minor who ascribed it to the gnostic Cerinthus.

Earlier in that century Papias of Hierapolis (A.D. 70?–140?) had indicated in *The Sayings of the Lord Explained* (a lost work in five books) that he knew John's gospel, as hinted at by Eusebius[2] and testified to by Jerome and other later fathers.[3] Justin (d. ca. 165), who calls the gospels "memoirs of the apostles,"[4] seems to have known John's *logos* doctrine[5] and in one place quotes the fourth gospel.[6] He attributes the millenarian teaching of Revelation (20:4–10) to "John, one of the apostles of Christ."[7] Hippolytus of Rome (d. 235) makes the same attribution of the two books to John in a work no longer extant, *On the Gospel of John and the Apocalypse,* rebutting Gaius of Rome over the Johannine authorship of Revelation.[8]

Valentinus whom St. Irenaeus describes as an Egyptian was the founder of a school at Rome in the mid-second century. In his theogonic and cosmogonic speculations he made much of the prologue of Jn (1:1–18) and had a disciple, Heracleon, who probably after 150 wrote the first, very detailed commentary on the gospel. Origen (d. 253–4) preserved many fragments of Heracleon's work in his own commentary which disclose the allegorical hermeneutics of the gnostic thinker. Thus, for example, the Samaritan woman represents the pneumatic elect; Abraham, Moses, and Jacob the demiurge; and her being told by Jesus to call her husband a revelation that, in her husband-less condition, she has a "plērōma," a "husband in the aiōn," who is her syzygos (the one to whom she is paired).[9] Irenaeus, Clement of Alexandria, and Origen found this type of exegesis contrived but it continued to be popular in Christian gnostic circles, casting a shadow on the FG's orthodoxy. Some Christians even rejected Jn as heretical. Valentinus' disciples produced a *Gospel of Truth,* not presumably the same as the Coptic meditation on salvation of the same name from Nag Hammadi, which evidently served as a kind of shadowy counterpart to the FG.

With Irenaeus' acceptance of Jn in his *Five Books against Gnōsis, Falsely So-Called* (*Adversus Haereses*) there was expressed the first indisputable claim of apostolic authorship: "Lastly John, the disciple of the Lord, who also lay on his breast, himself published the gospel, while he was staying at Ephesus in Asia."[10]

The differences between Jn and the synoptics are so marked, chiefly the extended discourses of Jesus and the little use of biographical incidents in common, apart from the baptism, the miraculous feeding and walking on water, and the passion and risen life narratives, that a way around the problem was arrived at early. Clement of Alexandria wrote:

> Last of all John, perceiving that the external facts (*ta sōmatika*) had been made plain in the gospels, being urged by his friends and inspired by the Spirit . . . composed a spiritual gospel (*pneumatikon . . . euaggelion*).[11]

Origen echoed this explanation by observing in his *Commentary on John* at 10.4–6 that strict historical accuracy had to be abandoned because of the needs of spiritual truth. Something like this attempt to account for the differences has continued down to our own time with the popular, conventional view that John presumed a knowledge of the synoptic details in his hearers and proceeded to present it differently for the sake of deeper understanding. Until recently the opinion prevailed in learned circles that Jn is untrustworthy historically because it is so concerned with theology. A discussion went on concurrently as to whether the author of Jn knew the synoptics or only the materials on which they drew. His use of the Marcan order, even to certain small details, and of Lucan data and development in the passion account heightened the debate.

Some John Scholarship of the Years Before World War II: Hoskyns

Any report on "what they are saying about John" needs a starting point, probably best arrived at by "what they *were* saying."

For that, an account of certain landmark books produced between 1940 and twenty years ago seems to be in order. Those will include the commentaries of Hoskyns and Davey,[12] Bultmann,[13] Barrett,[14] the two thematic explorations of Dodd[15] and finally the commentaries of Schnackenburg[16] and Brown.[17] Any number of other commentaries likewise appeared in that period or shortly thereafter, notably those of Braun,[18] Lindars,[19] and Haenchen,[20] but they will not be summarized here. Readers of this book can profitably consult Robert Kysar's examination of Johannine scholarship for the period 1955–75 (at this writing out of print), brought up to date in a not so readily accessible bibliographical tool,[21] and before that a 1955 updating of a summary by British scholar W.F. Howard.[22]

Sir Edwyn Hoskyns of Cambridge worked on his commentary on Jn for fourteen years. At his death in 1937 he left six completed chapters ready for the press and another seventeen in rough form. These Francis Noel Davey published in a book of 604 pages.[23] Hoskyns seems to have relied most on Adolf Schlatter's commentary of 1930. He takes no position on the authorship of Jn except to assume, more than argue, that the same person wrote the Johannine epistles, probably somewhere in Syria. For Hoskyns the ultimate authority underlying the Johannine writings was theological. They were addressed to people who had a great deal of miscellaneous information about the Lord's life ("episodic" is his description of the synoptic gospels, documents that he does not think the author of the FG possessed). John saw that the tradition had an underlying meaning, "peering out of it at every point, a meaning which is 'beyond history', and which alone makes sense of history. To disclose this underlying history of the tradition he wrote his gospel."[24] The gospel was written for Christians and contained a polemic against Jews but was not directed against Ebionites, Gnostics, or any other group. The author wants his hearers to go behind him and the church to the apostles, and behind them to the visible, historical Jesus. Behind Jesus lies the glory of the Son of God, the Word. But Jn and the church and Jesus are ultimately meant to rest in God, who was self-manifested—given as an epiphany to the world—in this Son.

The matrix of the gospel with its constant reference to the

Hebrew scriptures and Palestinian geography was Jewish, not Christian or Mandean-Gnostic. Hoskyns knew an article of Rudolf Bultmann from 1925, prompted by the researches of orientalist M. Lidzbarski, claiming that a gnostic redeemer-myth with the Baptist at its center underlay the Johannine prologue. This he rejected along with the primary influence of Hellenic thought on the gospel, although "the Evangelist may have recognized that the Christian teaching concerning the Word of God had further implications for Greeks familiar with the Stoic conception of the divine Logos or Person."[25] Hoskyns entertains no scruple about speaking of the Jews' "national rejection of Christ" (p. 273; sometimes "the Jewish authorities"), hence the Jews as the targets of the FG without further nuance.

The commentary that follows each pericope of the gospel in the Revised Version (1881) makes extensive use of philological arguments from the critical readings of the text that Hoskyns defends, and the church fathers. The erudition of the part labeled "Commentary" is impressive. The reflections that immediately follow the Bible text are theological and at times meditative in the best homiletical style. There are numerous "Detached Notes" throughout, for example the one on Jn 1:13 which provides all the arguments for and against a singular rather than a plural reading, "who was born not of bloods," etc., making it not believers born of God but Jesus virginally born of Mary. Here Hoskyns simply provides the (weak) textual evidence and surprisingly strong patristic support of the idea, leaving the reader to conclude wrongly that the evidence against the plural reading (the blood of Joseph and Mary as the deduction) was overwhelming. The subsequent consensus goes against Hoskyns on textual grounds, seeing in the threefold denial (despite the "bloods") an affirmation of Jesus' childhood of God by divine initiative through faith. While the observations on the individual vignettes and discourses of Jesus are fraught with learned detail, Hoskyns ventures that the encounter of the church with the Spirit through the person of Jesus is the overarching theme for the whole gospel. The synoptic use of traditional eschatological terms has become, "in an evolution of perception," a conscious theological language of the Spirit. The "urgent, final impact of God upon the world" which eschatology is concerned to proclaim "is now expressed as theology," a theology inherent in the Marcan reminiscences of a generation before.[26] As to the historical character of the gospel, Hoskyns assumes that everything somehow happened in Jesus' life as reported in the FG, while acknowledging the impossibility of distinguishing history from interpretation. His Introduction allows the possibility that historical occurrences may be given a symbolic value in Jn but this is not much adverted to in his subsequent exegeses. The relation of the FG to the earlier tradition of the synoptics and before absorbs most of his energies.

The Influential Work of Bultmann

Rudolf Bultmann altered the course of Johannine studies radically in a book published while Germany was at war (1941). Hoskyns' work had been produced between World War I and the Great Depression but its impact, like Bultmann's, was not felt until after World War II. Bultmann's *The Gospel of John* leaps immediately into 70 pages of commentary on the book's first 18 verses without introduction. There the reader is introduced to the Marburg scholar's two main convictions: that a cultic community hymn based on a pre-Christian gnostic redeemer-myth underlies the prologue (1:1–18), part of a collection of gnostic "revelation-discourses" which are the basis of the Jesus-discourses in the gospel,[27] and that the FG should be read existentially as promising man (*Mensch*) freedom from death, "the fate that makes existence sheerly unintelligible."[28] Jesus' prime function as the Son is to be the Revealer of God. God's glory (*doxa*) is manifested in history in the word become flesh, a word that brings the knowledge of God that Jesus both speaks and himself *is*.[29]

Bultmann does not believe that the evangelist is committed to the metaphysical dualism between matter and spirit that he finds in his gnostic source. The "evangelist" designates the penultimate writer who framed a gospel that the "editor" later presented to the church. The spirit-matter dualism concept of gnosticism, like that of the preexistence of souls and other aspects of the myth, is edited out. For Bultmann, Jesus is a human figure "pure and simple," the revealer of the glory of God who is uniquely God's Son. Jesus as Logos is a salvific intermediary between God and the world in the same way that the gnostic Wisdom is, on whom that late biblical equivalent of torah draws. Personified Wisdom, in Bultmann's view, is drawn from pagan myth.

None of the arguments leveled against Bultmann, which maintain that all the "gnostic influences" on Jn he cites were post-Johannine (among them the Odes of Solomon, the letters of Ignatius, the Christian gnostic corpus, and the Hermetic and Mandean literatures), dislodged his conviction that a well formulated revealer-redeemer myth lay behind the gospel we have in hand. The "revelation-discourses source" that drew on the myth, produced in poetic-sounding Aramaic, was one major building-block of the gospel. The other was the "signs-source," a collection of synoptic-like miracle stories distinct from those of the synoptic traditions. For narrative elements in stories such as those of Nicodemus, the Samaritan woman, and the man blind from birth, the evangelist acted creatively, drawing on "miscellaneous sources": snatches of reminiscence, parables of Jesus, and the like. The fourth source posited is a "passion and risen-life source" that came to the evangelist in semitized Greek.

The Way the Evangelist Used His Four Sources

Bultmann's major project, perhaps, was to identify the evangelist as the weaver of his sources into a continuous narrative to which an editor gave final shape. This was done by assuming that the materials that lay behind the gospel were each of them perfectly consistent in vocabulary and style. Any abrupt transitions, therefore, in the present gospel or any passages uncharacteristic of the evangelist's editorial style signal the insertion of material from a source. Put in reverse, the characteristics of each source are so distinctive that each of the sources can be separated out. Thus, the "incongruities in the relationship of a passage to its context are the basic means of detecting the sources, the evangelist, and the redactor [editor] (context criticism)."[30]

To choose an example: Bultmann finds it clear that Jn 1:22–24 are an insertion by the editor into the text of the evangelist. It is the evangelist's idea that the Baptist is but a witness to Jesus who is a prophet and the Christ.[31] The three verses break the continuity between vv. 21 and 25 of the source because the Baptist's denials of who he is (vv. 20–21) are not logically followed by the characterization of him in vv. 22–24. Hence, an ecclesiastical editor who knew the traditional use of Is 40:3 must have inserted it at this point. Further, v. 26 should clearly be followed by v. 31 because, linked together by the verb "know," they answer the question put in v. 25, "If you are not the Messiah, nor Elijah, nor the Prophet, why do you baptize?"

> V. 27 is again an additional comment from the Synoptic tradition (Mk 1.7 par.); v. 28 on the other hand is the original conclusion of the section[1] [[1] cp. the conclusions 6:59; 8:20; 12:36) and originally came after v. 34. Vv. 29–30 are connected with v. 28. The misplacing of vv. 28–30 can be attributed only to the disorder of the text which the editor had before him.[32]

The section ends with the "original text of the Gospel" in Greek, with appropriate verse numbers, in the following sequence: 1:1, 20, 21, 25, 26, 31, 33, 34, 28, and "(There follow vv. 29–30)."[33] Something similar is done with the "original" order of chs. 4—6 (4, 6, 5)[34] and 13–17 ("13.1–30 records Jesus' last meal with his disciples; 17.1–26 gives us the farewell prayer; 13.31–35; 15.1—16.33; 13.36—14.31 contain the farewell discourses and conversations").[35]

It would be a mistake to think that Bultmann's theory of the ingenious and complex composition of the gospel in its present form was his chief contribution to its study. It is true that he solved many problems posed by the *aporias* (awkward transitions) that abound in Jn. But the theory of a signs-source that he based on a 1922 article of A. Faure in *ZNW*[36] is his contribution that remains. His theory that the evangelist likewise drew on a discourses-source has largely yielded to one that sees the evangelist himself as the composer of Jesus' discourses. Kysar presents in schematic form the contents that five later authors assign to the signs-source. Two of them, Teeple and Fortna, think that a passion- or passion-resurrection source was a part of it.[37]

The Consensus of the 1980s on Bultmann's Composition Theory

Important as Bultmann's work on sources has been to Johannine scholarship, it has led to a verdict of "not proven" with respect to any but a signs-source. His inability to convince large numbers that the evangelist possessed a gnostic redeemer-myth that he reworked, placing Jesus at the center, derived as much from the intricacy of the editorial process he assumed as from doubts that such a pre-Christian myth existed. In his apodicticism, his certitude that a herald of the gospel would so deliver himself over to a pagan literary composition, lay his failure.

Where Bultmann succeeded was in identifying the evangelist's theological project. This was, first, in chs. 3—12 to portray the revelation of God's glory to the world in Jesus—the struggle between light and darkness hinted at in 1:5, 9–11. The result of this epiphany was *krisis* in the sense of both "judgment" and "division." Chs. 13—20 portray the revelation of the "glory" to believers, or the victory of the light, thereby illustrating 1:12-18.[38]

The final editor's ecclesial concern with the sacraments of baptism and eucharist, which Bultmann categorizes as Hellenist in origin and trivial relative to the gospel's message of belief in the Son, is another *a priori* of the Marburger, like that of the redeemer myth.

His formidable knowledge of pagan Greek and Christian sectarian writings commands respect, although in rabbinic matters he is often confined to what Strack-Billerbeck's anthology tells him. His command of the exegetical literature had no parallel in Johannine scholarship up to his time. This, plus his firm grasp on the overall design of the evangelist, continues to make his commentary worth consulting before anything more recent is looked at. His individualist interpretations of a message directed at a believing *people* and his insensitivity to the Jewish character of Christianity, as if that aspect were somehow related to Jn's *Ioudaioi*, can be looked past. Bultmann has many insightful things to say about light and darkness in Jn, faith and unbelief, the intimate relation between the Father and the Son, and of both to those who believe in him.

The English Tradition in Johannine Studies, Continued

C.K. Barrett reports in the Preface to the second edition of his *The Gospel according to St. John* that it was rejected from a series for its length and detail but rescued for the publisher SPCK by the good offices of F.N. Davey.[39] Seeing it as a "juvenile work" twenty-three years later, he acknowledges he has learned much from later commentators but by his own account has adopted few new positions. Barrett thinks that Mk is a source for Jn and that Lk probably is too in a smaller degree; Jn deliberately reworked sayings and incidents from the two in light of his overall purpose. This was to set forth the traditional faith in a new idiom, to strengthen those unsettled by winds of gnostic doctrine, to win new converts, and to provide a more adequate exposition of the faith itself.[40] Qumrân does not unlock much in Jn, nor can the historical traditions discernible in it be readily disentangled from the interpretive comments. For Barrett a discourse-source is even less provable than a signs-source and a Jerusalem-source is not likely at all. The Johannine passion story is an edited version of the Marcan into which Jn has introduced some fresh material. Theories of displacement and subsequent redaction create as many problems as they solve. It is doubtful, finally, whether Q ever existed.

John knew the Septuagint, the Hebrew Bible, apocalyptic Judaism and rabbinic exegesis, popular Platonic-Stoic teaching and the light/life material that would emerge in the 2nd–4th c. *Hermetica*. Barrett finds in Philo the best witness to pre-Christian gnosis, which "plays some part in the make-up of Johannine thought."[41] John fused Jewish and Hellenist elements into "a unitary presentation of the universal significance of Jesus,"[42] laying both Jewish thought and Greek metaphysics under tribute in his christology. Whereas the synoptics "simply view Jesus in the light of the eschatological crisis which he precipitated . . . John releases himself from a purely apocalyptic interpretation of Jesus, while he continues to use eschatological language (though not exclusively)."[43] He presents Jesus as the first creator and the final judge, the ultimate truth both of

God and of humanity, the image of God and the archetype of humanity, an ontological mediator between God and man. Jesus himself is the bearer of the Spirit; he also bestows the Spirit, the power at work in the church's mission and the source of its authority. The Spirit works by revealing the truth and relating the church positively to the truth upon which it stands. By so doing, this Spirit reacts negatively upon the world, which is judged.[44]

Barrett sees no opposition between "the disciple whom Jesus loved" (13:23; 19:26f.; 20:2; 21:7, 20) and the twelve, to whom he probably belonged. For the University of Durham scholar John the son of Zebedee, who was not the evangelist, was probably that beloved disciple. He migrated to Ephesus and died there, leaving behind an unnamed follower who composed chs. 1—20. Another disciple of John wrote the Apocalypse from John's authentic works. Probably two disciples wrote 1 Jn and 2 and 3 Jn. The author of Jn 21 sought to establish the association of Peter and the beloved disciple as partners, neither taking precedence. Peter is the head of the evangelistic and pastoral work of the church but the beloved disciple is the guarantor of its tradition regarding Jesus.[45]

Perhaps the strongest feature of the commentary, which may also be its enduring worth, is its careful attention to the manuscript witness or state of the text. Second in importance to these attempts to establish the product of the final redactor is Barrett's grammatical concern. Arguing both on his own and from authority, he debates constantly the renderings that ambiguities in the Greek will admit and votes on how to settle them. The same is true of John's style on the basis of word-count, grammatical construction, and parallel usages from the time. The notes on individual verses tend to satisfy in the wealth of background they provide.

Barrett adopts the view that "When all has been reviewed it is difficult to resist the impression that the Palestinian material has been disposed according to the demands of a dominant non-Jewish partner."[46] Studies of the last fifty years have concluded that not everything Jewish in the first century was Palestinian and that Palestine was not free of weighty Hellenist influence. Barrett may be the last of a long line of Johannine scholars to think that in Jn the non-Jewish partner dominated.

A Congregationalist Scholar Follows Upon a Methodist

C.H. Dodd's *The Interpretation of the Fourth Gospel* is too early for adequate treatment within this survey.[47] Its importance lay in its exploration of the background of the fourth gospel—which needed an inquiry that was not antecedently committed as Bultmann's was. Dodd coupled his research into possible literary and religious influences with a presentation of twelve leading ideas in Jn and a breakdown of its argument and structure. The Hermetic corpus of Greek writings from Egypt, in which Poimandres (a "Shepherd") is the divine revealer, shows how important the pagans considered knowledge of God to salvation and how widespread the conception was of the deity as life and light. The gnostic systems exposed by Irenaeus and Hippolytus, who were later to be sustained in their general accuracy by the Nag Hammadi finds of 1945 in Upper Egypt, are seen as derived from Oriental mythology more than Hellenic or Hebraic origins. Dodd showed that the formulation of a gnostic myth as complete in the pre-Christian period remains as much a matter of speculation as when Reitzenstein first posited it. The two books of the Mandeans, moreover (*Manda d'Hayye* = "Knowledge of Life"), a gnostic offshoot, are shown to go back no further than A.D. 700, whatever the age of their claim that John the Baptist was their founder. Lidzbarski's theory, seized upon by Reitzenstein and Bultmann, that an Iranian redemption myth underlay the religion of followers of the Baptist (see Acts 18:24—19:7), from which Christianity derived, is shown to be highly doubtful, not least because the Christian heresiologists are silent about the Mandaeans from the first century to the eighth.

Dodd's thematic study of Johannine symbolism under leading ideas such as eternal life, knowledge of God, truth, spirit, and logos, and light, glory, and judgment, was very helpful to readers confined to English language scholarship four decades ago. This was especially true because it never left biblical or pseudepigraphic sources aside while paying attention to Philonic and other Hellenic developments. Dodd's synthesis shed light on the rich religious vocabulary available to John without the evangelist's having to draw directly on this or that "source." Well past the midpoint of the book the gospel begins to be dealt with chapter by chapter, under the threefold heading, The Proem (1:1–18 prologue and 10–51 testimony), The Book of Signs (chs. 2–12) and The Book of the Passion (chs. 13–20 with ch. 21 as a postscript). The Book of Signs is divided into seven episodes, not all of them with a miracle at the core, and an epilogue. They are: The New Beginning, 2:1–4:42; The Life Giving Word, 4:46–5:47; Bread of Life, 6; Light and Life: Manifestation and Rejection, 7—8; Judgment by the Light, 9:1—10:21 with appendix, 10:22-39; The Victory of Life over Death, 11:1–53; Life through Death: The Meaning of the Cross, 12:1–36; and, as a postscript to these eleven chapters, 12:37-50. The chief insight of this first book of Dodd's is that provided by chs. 2—4, where the inauguration of new order of life in the enfleshed Word is examined in a succession of symbols of newness: new wine, new worship, new birth, a new bridegroom, new life-giving water, a new people where there had been two, and new life—all enclosed by a first sign (2:11) and a second (4:54).

Dodd's second volume, *Historical Tradition in the Fourth Gospel,* was published a decade later.[48] The author describes it as an expansion of the Appendix to the earlier work, "Some Considerations upon the Historical Aspect of the Fourth Gospel."[49] There he had written:

> The use of freely composed speeches to elucidate the significance of events does not in itself impugn the historical character of the narrative in the Fourth Gospel, any more than in Thucydides or Tacitus. There is however good reason to suspect that in some cases and in some respects the narratives which provide the setting for such speeches may have been moulded by the ideas which they are made to illustrate.[50]

Maintaining as established by form criticism that the narratives of the first three gospels have been thus molded, Dodd holds that there is no more reason to deny an historical character to the FG than to attribute a large measure of historicity to the synoptics. The topographical references in Jn (Sychar, Ephraim, Bethany beyond Jordan and six others) can scarcely have been inserted, he thinks, for symbolic reasons. But when, in this second volume, he

meticulously analyzes the Johannine passages most closely related
to the synoptic materials, he concludes that Jn (at least in 13:16;
12:25; 13:20; 20:23) "is not dependent on the Synoptic Gospels,
but is transmitting independently a special form of the common
oral tradition.[51] His conclusion, which is based on the accumula-
tion of probabilities is that

> behind the Fourth Gospel lies an ancient tradition inde-
> pendent of the other gospels, and meriting serious consid-
> eration as a contribution to our knowledge of the histori-
> cal facts concerning Jesus Christ. . . . All through I have
> assumed that the tradition we are trying to track down
> was oral . . . [although] written sources may have inter-
> vened between the strictly oral tradition and our Fourth
> Gospel.[52]

Dodd thinks it may be said of this pre-canonical tradition that
it shows contact with an Aramaic tradition ("The evangelist himself was probably a speaker of Aramaic"), that it appears "to point
to a Jewish (Jewish-Christian) setting," and that it retains allusions
to well-attested Jewish beliefs and has points of contact with Jewish
tradition. In summary, "The basic tradition . . . on which the evangelist is working was shaped (it appears) in a Jewish-Christian
environment still in touch with the synagogue, in Palestine, at a
relatively early date, at any rate before the rebellion of A.D.
66. . . . Yet there are in places signs of development either at a
later date or outside Palestine, or both."[53] To examine those conclusions carefully is to see that the Jewishness of the gospel is taken as
a sign of proximity to the actual events narrated, that "the tradition" is basically a matter of historicity, and that a leap has been
made from the text of Jn and the synoptics back to a pre-literary,
oral tradition—two distinct traditions, in fact—on which the first
written collections of sayings and stories were based.

John's Gospel as a Witness to the Events of History

Whatever else may be said of Dodd's *Historical Tradition*, he
is to be thanked for his exhaustive analysis of Johannine passages

where the wording is similar to that of any of the synoptics and where the underlying ideas are related, whether the relationship be close or tenuous. He does this by starting with the passion narrative under seven headings because there the likenesses are closest. Summing up after 150 pages of sifting the similarities, he concludes that there is no sufficient evidence to prove a literary dependence of the gospel of John on the others in this part of the gospel. "On the contrary there is cumulative evidence that the Johannine version represents (subject to some measure of 'writing up' by the evangelist) an independent strain of the common oral tradition, differing from the strains of tradition underlying Mark (Matthew) and Luke, though controlled by the same general *schema*."[54] Interestingly, Dodd takes the exchange between Jesus and Pilate (Jn 18:28–19:16) as evidence of Jn's boldness, as it represents Jesus' condemnation to be the result of a clash between his claims and those of Caesar. Dodd even permits himself to wonder if "We have no king but Caesar" was a profession of Jewish loyalty at the place where the gospel was written, as contrasted with a less than full allegiance by the followers of Jesus in the same locality. He writes: "I could much more easily believe that the Synoptists have reduced the political element in the tradition that had come down to them."[55] Granting the likelihood of "a certain amount of elaboration" in the two hearings before Pilate *in camera*, Dodd thinks that "it remains probable that the tradition upon which this elaboration was based . . . may well have been in some respects more fully informed [than Mark's]."[56]

Dealing with the ministry of Jesus as the second narrative portion of Jn by proceeding backward from the passion, and the story of the Baptist and the first disciples as the third portion, *Historical Tradition* concludes that John, Mark and Luke used separate strands of tradition for the anointing stories,[57] and that the healing stories of Jn had no common nucleus with those of the synoptics.[58] A traditional narrative underlies Jn's account of the resuscitation of Lazarus, which has been shaped in the course of Christian preaching and teaching. John has "remoulded [it] to convey his own special message,"[59] even as Mk has done with his distinct healing and resuscitation traditions. The tradition on the Baptist in Jn "included very primitive material, but before it reached our evangelist it had undergone development in the environment indicated (viz., one in which Christians claimed the Baptist as the first 'confessor' of Jesus, made long before the gospel was written)."[60] Dodd finds seven sayings of Jesus that are parabolic in form (7:24; 16:21; 11:9–10; 8:35; 10:1–5; 3:29; 5:19–20a). "Yet in no case is there the remotest likelihood of derivation from Synoptic sources."[61] And so the whole work concludes that in every instance cited or explored Jn is found to have reached back to "a very early form of tradition indeed . . . making it the point of departure for his profound theological reinterpretation."[62] But that traditional source is never the one that is drawn on by the synoptics.

The chief impression left by the meticulous and at times tedious word study of this book is that the author is unwilling to depart from the earlier conventional wisdom that an evangelist was above all an editor of received traditions. When one of them—apart from Mt's obvious editing of Mk's and Lk's less evident efforts, and the incorporation of Q sayings by Lk and Mt—engages in the pure genius of authorship, it is grudgingly acknowledged as a brief patch of elaboration or composition. A second absentee from the discussion is the lively role played by orality in first-century composition. The evangelists are assumed to have been seated in studies surrounded by the LXX, the Masoretic Text, several targums, and numerous scraps of written gospel tradition to which the oral had been reduced. But this is an imposition of twentieth century scholarly methods on the first century.[65] A writer like the evangelist John would have had endless passages of the Bible committed to memory, both exactly and inexactly. He would have known how he had been accustomed to proclaim the gospel over decades without being able to cite all the ways in which traditions had come to him. Faced with this writing challenge the evangelist, as distinct from the final editor, might have sought out some written sources he had not consulted in years—like anyone in the literary game. Of the heavy dependence of any ancient writer on heard, memorized, and spoken transmission as contrasted with the careful copying out of written sources, there is no clue in Dodd.

A U.S. Scholar Enters the Lists

Raymond E. Brown's *The Gospel According to John* was published in 1966 and 1970, as indicated above (n. 17). Numerous section-references to the second volume as well as numbered Appendixes appeared in the first, indicating that the whole work already existed in some, if not final, form. The two Jn volumes are of 538 and 670 pages, the first preceded by an Introduction that runs to 145. Apart from its exhaustive reference to Johannine literature (well beyond that in English and German) and its balanced judgments, the commentary recommends itself for its clarity of exposition and pattern of organization. The Introduction in ten numbered parts deals with subjects such as the unity and composition of the Fourth Gospel, the tradition behind it, proposed influences on its religious thought, the destination and purpose of the gospel, and the identity of the author and its place of composition. An eleventh part is a general selective bibliography of twenty-eight works that were actually used, none older than 1928 besides Loisy and Schürer. As one reaches the commentary proper (forty-five sections in the first volume, thirty-eight in the second), one finds first the translation of a pericope, then notes that are chiefly observations on words and phrases, often raising questions to be resolved in the third part headed "Comment." This is frequently divided into "General" and "Specific" (sometimes "Detailed"), but not in the case of shorter pericopes such as i 29–34 (dealt with in section 3) or the four pericopes and their comments into which vi 1–34 are broken. The Greek and Hebrew are transliterated into English, something Dodd did not do (nor with Syriac!). Bibliographies are provided at the end of each section, and outlines of what to expect in the gospel precede them. These pedagogic helps, glossaries in the appendixes, and charts comparing Jn with the synoptics (as in the multiplication of the loaves and the Barabbas incident) make this commentary a very usable tool indeed.

A Theory of Composition That Has Come To Prevail

A feature found in the Introduction that has proved durable over the last twenty-five years is Brown's theory of the five stages of Jn's composition, two pre-literary and three in its written form. These are: (1) a collection of traditional materials containing the words and works of Jesus, independent in origin from the synoptic tradition(s); (2) oral preaching and teaching over several decades that molded the tradition in the form and style that came to characterize the FG: short dramas worked up around Jesus' miracles (including the now familiar Johannine misunderstandings and ironies); lengthy discourses devised by members of a school that had one principal preacher; toward the end of this second stage, written forms of what was preached and taught; (3) the material from stage 2 woven into the first edition of a consecutive gospel, the work of a master teacher and theologian; (4) a second edition (and possibly more) by this same evangelist to meet the objections or difficulties of groups like followers of the Baptist, believers in Jesus associated with the synagogue, and others; (5) a final editing or redaction not always easily distinguishable from stage 4, most likely by a disciple of the evangelist and part of his school: chs. 15–17 added to Jesus' supper discourse with 16:4–33 a variant duplicate of ch. 15, likewise the Lazarus story (chs. 11 and 12 possibly added at stages 4 or 5), an insertion that could have caused the shift of the cleansing of the temple to ch. 2; the eucharistic words of Jesus at the supper placed in ch. 6, thus associating the two events with a different Passover from the final one in stage 4. In all, the final redactor, like the evangelist in his second edition, used additional materials developed within the Johannine school.

Brown had called ch. 21 an Epilogue in his early outline and identifies it in his second volume as the work of the redactor of chs. 1–20 or perhaps another. This editor, who is not the evangelist and who has more ancient material to add, is certainly not Bultmann's Ecclesiastical Redactor whose outlook on church and sacraments is thought to be quite foreign to that of the evangelist.[66]

Brown gives his reasons for thinking that the gospel in its present form was written between 80 and 110, probably toward 100 and in Ephesus (where Revelation was the more primitive product of the Johannine school) rather than Alexandria or Antioch. As to authorship, he finds it hard to argue against the unanimous external testimony that it was the work of John, son of Zebedee. He also thinks

John the best candidate for "the disciple whom Jesus loved" (over Lazarus, John Mark, or an unknown disciple, surely not one other than a member of the synoptics' twelve). On internal evidence, there is the attribution of the gospel tradition to an eyewitness disciple in 19:35; cf. 21:24, which attributes testimony to "these things" (ch. 21? the whole gospel?) to the disciple whom Jesus loved of v. 20. He is obviously the same person as the one at the foot of the cross in 19:26 but also distinguished from the "we" of 21:24 who wrote ch. 21. There are six references in all to the disciple whom Jesus loved, designated BD by Brown for "beloved disciple": 13:23–26; 19:25–27; 20:2–10; 21:7, 21–23 (with reference back to 13:23–26); 21:24 ("this same disciple" as "witness for these things"). Once, "another disciple . . . known to the high priest" is spoken of with Peter (18:15–16) while "the one Jesus loved" of 21:2–10 is also called "the other disciple." Brown thinks it plausible that "an (the) other disciple" is this person's self-designation while his status as beloved of Jesus is the work of his own followers. No one seems to Brown more likely than the disciple John to be the one who has preserved his memories of Jesus and was closely associated with Peter. The son of Zebedee could well have been Jesus' first cousin, son of Salome, Jesus' mother's sister (see the note on 19:25).

Brown faces the formidable difficulties raised against his position by stating initially that almost every account of the composition from the patristic period associates others with John. The apostle cannot have been the final redactor of stage 5 because the "we" of 21:24 is distinct from the BD, who was also probably dead when the chapter was written (see vv. 22–23). But he could have been and "probably [was] the source of the historical tradition behind the Fourth Gospel."[67] More than the source, in his preaching he "would necessarily have had to adapt to his audience the tradition of which he was a living witness."[68] So much for stage 1, but was he responsible for stages 2 through 4? For these he provided guidance and encouragement, especially to the "*one principal disciple* whose transition of the historical material received from John was marked with dramatic genius and profound theological insight, and it is the preaching and teaching of this disciple which gave shape to the stories and discourses now found in the

Fourth Gospel."[69] Brown gives this disciple-evangelist no name
but notes that some may be attracted by the hypothesis of John the
Presbyter, named by Papias ca. 130.

Some Further Positions of Brown

While acknowledging that Jn's revelatory discourses are not
Greek poetry or semitic, in Burney's back-translation into Aramaic, Brown describes his search for the format into which he set
these discourses in English translation. Bultmann had done the
same arranging of lines in Greek, and Donatien Mollat in French
for *La Bible de Jérusalem,* but the problems are obviously different
in each language. Consulting those three and the earlier attempt of
Gächter, Brown found the principles of division entirely flexible,
and hence proceeded to render the quasi-poetic prose ("solemn
[but] far from lyrical. . . . [a repetition achieving] monotonous
grandeur") into sense lines in ordinary English resembling the non-
literary Greek.

In treating the opening verses of Jn (1:1–18) Brown takes
them to be a Christ-hymn composed in the Johannine church. He
compares it to the hymns of Phil 2:6–11, Col 1:15–20 and 1 Tim
3:16 and finds them not dissimilar. Opting for the verses that constituted the original hymn is not easy; among the eight authors whose
choices he cites, no two make the same. Brown votes, tentatively,
for four strophes composed of vv. 1–2, 3–5, 10–12b, and 14, 15, a
reconstruction unlike any of the other eight. An editor, he thinks,
has inserted the prose account about the preaching of John into the
poem (vv. 6–9, 12c–14, 16) but he finds "interesting" the suggestion of Boismard and others that the gospel originally began with,
"There was sent by God a man named John" (as in the Samson
narrative of Judges) into which the hymn was intercalated.

As to the Word of the prologue, it is a divine communication
to humanity in which the messenger himself is the message. The
opening words of Genesis repeated here "are peculiarly fitting to
open the account of what God has said and done in the new dispen-
sation."[70] The career of the Word in the world has empowered
people to become God's children (v. 12), something heretofore
unachievable (in the sense of their being begotten from above by

the Spirit of Jesus; 3:15). The rejection of the Word by men in v. 10 ("his own people," in v. 11) has no anti-Jewish overtones for Brown, being quite like the human rejection of Wisdom in Enoch 42:2: "Wisdom came to make her dwelling among human offspring and found no dwelling place." Similarly, "the Jews" is used interchangeably with the chief priests and the Pharisees as "almost a technical title for *the religious authorities, particularly those in Jerusalem, who are hostile to Jesus.*"[71] "Israel" is Jn's favorable term, "the Jews" often although not always his unfavorable term (chs. 11–12 constitute an exception, where he holds it means Judeans). Brown thinks that by the time the FG was written in its final form the Jews who believed in Jesus would no longer have been designated as Jews, nor does the law any longer affect them.[72]

As part of this there is his conviction, held by W.D. Davies and others, that the Eighteen Benedictions were reformulated ca. 85 so that the twelfth "was a curse on the *minim* or heretics, primarily Jewish-Christian."[73] Recited publicly it was thus a trap calculated to make believers in Jesus curse themselves, much like Edward Everett Hale's fictitious Philip Nolan choking on the recitation of Scott's *Innominatus* on shipboard. Important to this outlook is the supposition that the seemingly technical term *aposynágōgos* (*-oi*) of 9:22, 12:42 and 16:2 came closest in meaning to total ejection from Israel toward the end of the first century.[74] The separation of Christians from Jews as a distinct religious community is thus taken for granted within sixty years after the resurrection, on the further assumption that the decree of the academy at Yavneh was acted upon throughout the Mediterranean Jewish world.

As Brown proceeds through an exhaustive interpretation of the mini-dramas and discourses that go to make up Jn he expounds fully the critical theories with which he cannot agree. This he does so even-handedly that often, after he has presented three or four opinions, the reader cannot tell where he will come out. Unlike many exegetes he presents the views of church fathers of the east and west, which often prove surprisingly modern. The Catholic scholarship of Europe likewise gets a hearing it has not received in German- and British-dominated scholarship. If being "conservative" means taking seriously positions sanctioned by long-standing acceptance, Brown is conservative. He is, at the same time, occasionally as radical as any critic.[75] One thing the reader can count on regularly is his lack of enthusiasm for source criticism, understood as confidently assigning pericopes to written sources and not hesitating to identify their beginning or end, even if it should occur in mid-verse. He simply does not think the gospel came into existence by that careful stitching process. It was, rather, a compilation from a large Johannine pool, the work of a "school" which seemed to have as its primary conviction that nothing of the developed historical tradition should be lost. Displacements, awkward "seams" and the like did not bother the final redactor(s) so long as, in some fashion, it was all *there*.

Like Bultmann Brown is always worth consulting, even by those who are predisposed to find one right and the other wrong. Before these two vote on a phrase, a passage, or the gospel's whole drift, they give a hearing to massive amounts of evidence.

A Magisterial Work Appearing Shortly after Brown's

With Rudolf Schnackenburg, a Catholic professor at Würzburg, it is much the same as with Bultmann and Brown. The first volume of his commentary was published at the same time as Brown's and was completed over a ten-year period.[76] He draws on a wide range of northern European and British scholarship and is more venturesome than Brown in his reconstructions of the present text of Jn. He holds that chs. 5 and 6 originally occurred in reverse order, 7:15–24 coming after 5:47.[77] This sequence keeps Jesus in Galilee for the miracle of the loaves, ch. 6 following immediately on ch. 4, then presents a sabbath healing in Jerusalem (5:8) which triggers the clash that continues with growing intensity throughout the feast of Tabernacles. Schnackenburg like Brown supposes that the series of farewell discourses in chs. 15—17, all by the same author, were inserted after 14:31 by later editors who left the finality of that verse ("Come, then. Let us be on our way") intact. There are other displacements he identifies but cannot account for quite so readily, like 3:31–36 and 12:44–50. The first is clearly not an utterance of the baptizing prophet John, both because of its contents and because the evangelist, "contrary to a fairly widespread opinion, always marks off Jesus' discourses clearly."[78] Placing the segment of discourse after 3:21 would solve one problem but create others. As to the second pericope, 12:44–50, it is clearly anticlimactic to the final reflections contained in vv. 37–43 but is not easily situated in its proper place. Schnackenburg sees in Jn a writer who supposes in his readers a knowledge of several matters in the synoptic tradition but not known to them from it. Like Brown, he posits a substratum or early stage of the Johannine tradition which may be contemporaneous with the synoptic tradition. Jn's main interest is clear: "to delineate boldly the majestic figure of the eschatological bringer of revelation and salvation, to display the radiant glory of the Logos as he lives on earth and dwells among us, to disclose the ever- present significance of the saving events which lie in the past."[79]

Whoever "the evangelist" or basic author of Jn was, for Schnackenburg he did not write under gnostic influences of the kind that surface in the Nag Hammadi texts or Odes of Solomon. Neither must the idea that a simple Galilean fisherman could not have risen to the spiritual heights of the fourth gospel be accepted without question. The content, language, and thought of Jn point to a Hellenistic disciple of the apostle who committed it to writing, probably as the member of a school or evangelizing company, with the possible mediation of a venerable preacher responsible for the typical Johannine discourses of Jesus. Schnackenburg is sure that the BD was an historical, not a symbolic figure, but at first cannot come down firmly on the side of his having been the son of Zebedee or any other individual. This does not keep him from maintaining that the ancient apostolic authority behind Jn is Zebedee's son in the early stages of the tradition. Written sources to which Lk and even Mk had access could also have been influential. (Brown, incidentally, does not outlaw the possibility of a Johannine redactor's having known Mk's gospel.) Schnackenburg's ultimate decision on the BD is that the disciples of the apostle John, including the evangelist, would have been the ones accustomed to describing their master as "the disciple whom Jesus loved," substituting this reverential title for John's "I" in the early, oral stages of gospel composition.[80]

Schnackenburg on Jn's Purpose and Style

An examination of Johannine speech patterns is shown to disclose, on the whole, semitic rather than Greek rhetoric. (Schlatter's 1902 study assembling linguistic parallels to Jn in the Tannaitic-era Mekhilta on Exodus and Sifre on Deuteronomy are cited favorably, before a linguistic analysis of Johannine phrases having a semitic coloration is provided.) This includes the method of concentric or more properly spiral exposition of a subject. Schnackenburg shows the extent of Jn's familiarity with Pharisaic and Rabbinic Judaism as well as with language patterns that surface in the Qumrân texts. The author of Jn is said to be totally ignorant of Greco-Roman philosophy except for some terms that were in the public domain like *logos* and "re-birth." The evangelist's main interest is in belief in Jesus as messiah in a way that transcends all previous expectations (his pre-cosmic existence as Word not least); likewise, salvation by the exalted Christ as a present reality, expressed in a formula like "my flesh for the life of the world" (6:5); and intimate union with God through belief in Christ. He was above all a theologian who put the faith of his community in Jesus on the lips of Jesus.

As in any commentary, the author of this one seems to grow in sophistication and insight as he moves forward into the text. The technique of comment on verses and pericopes forbids a development of the evangelist's themes except for those places where the writer stops to make one. One finds in the first volume the familiar tendency to track down parallels to every word or phrase in the Bible, the apocrypha, or Qumrân, creating the impression that the author thinks the evangelist *could* have been influenced by these scraps. Reflections on what a total pericope might have signified to its framer is thus drowned in minute etymological detail. Format and style change in Volume 2, which appeared in German after a five-year interval. The bibliographical entries are much more current and on the target of the text. Those in Volume 1 give evidence of long-term hoarding without much culling as publication came on. The commentary also begins to consist of lengthy reflections on the pericopes under consideration, far better developed and less fragmented than before. Thus, one could encounter in the early volume a footnote of this sort, imposing Christian ideas of

Jesus as the messiah on an unsuspecting eighth and seventh centuries B.C.: "The enquiring Pharisees [of 1:24–26] must have known that the Holy Spirit was part of the Messianic blessings (cf. Ezek 36:25f.; 37:5f.; 39:29; Joel 3:1ff.; Is 32:15; 44:3; 59:21) and hence that a ritual merely of water fulfilled no Messianic function." Although blameless before John the Baptizer's appearance, Schnackenburg holds, they were surely at fault, on biblical grounds, in face of the preaching of Jesus.

Brown in a review of Schnackenburg wrote: "Thus far in the twentieth century this may well be the best full-scale commentary on a book of the New Testament written by a European Roman Catholic." One can concur in saying at least that much of Schnackenburg's achievement, perhaps more.

2
The Question of Sources

Rudolf Bultmann's 1941 commentary *The Gospel of John* provided a theory of the three major sources and an amorphous fourth on which the evangelist drew before the whole gospel was edited and drastically rearranged by an "Ecclesiastical Redactor." Eugen Ruckstuhl seemed to refute its major contentions effectively a decade later.[1] He maintained that there were no written sources, since Johannine characteristics could be shown to prevail throughout the fourth gospel. The question lay dormant until 1958 when Wilhelm Wilkens, another Swiss, proposed a basic signs gospel, the work of the beloved disciple, who also later redacted it and added discourse material.[2] In a final editing the existing text was rearranged and further added to, with a Passover framework imposed on the whole that had not been present initially (see 2:13; 6:4; 11:55, which are followed by narratives that do not seem to fit these introductions). Wilkens gave more attention than Bultmann to method by stressing the contextual evidence pointing to successive editings of an initial source.

Reconstructing the Signs-Source: Fortna

Meantime, Bultmann's one contention that survived with least challenge was that John had employed a "signs source" (SQ as he called it, for *Semeia-Quelle*). *Semeia* and sometimes *erga* ("works") were the terms in the FG for the miraculous deeds put forward in proof of Jesus' messiahship. Bultmann did not delineate them in any one place, referring to them in extended footnotes only as they occurred. D.M. Smith[3] submitted Bultmann's theory to a clear exposition and then critiqued it, but it remained for R.T. Fortna to do what Bultmann had failed to do. He provided a Greek text of the hypothetical signs-source, going farther than the master by finding it to be not merely a collection of miracle-stories but a true gospel.[4] It had no teaching of Jesus, he concluded, but it did culminate in a passion and resurrection narrative.

Eduard Schwartz of Tübingen early in this century appears to have been the first to apply the Greek term *aporia* (lit. "block," "obstruction") to the Johannine material. It describes "the many inconsistencies, disjunctures and hard connections, even contradictions—which the text shows, notably in the narrative portions."[5] Seeing in these editorial seams evidence of insertion of material into a source, Fortna went on the hypothesis that the present gospel was the (probably multiple) redaction of a basic text. Bultmann had provided him with a lead by identifying a tension between the actual accounts of Jesus' miraculous deeds (2:1–12; 4:46–54; 5:1–9, 6:1–13; 9:1–7; 11:1–44; 21:1–6) and the summaries and editorial comments that accompanied them. But Fortna observed that Bultmann brought preconceived theological and stylistic judgments into the discussion. Fortna thought this improper and confined himself to internal criteria. The chief criterion he employed was the existence of aporias in the miracle stories (reckoning the walking on water, 6:15–25, as one of them, as Bultmann had not). These he thought could best be explained as indicators of Johannine additions to a pre-Johannine source. Also, using the stylistic criteria of Ruckstuhl and Schweizer, he came to an opposite conclusion from theirs, namely that the signs source was marked by peculiarities of language and style. This hypothetical source is more akin to synoptic style than Johannine. Since it contains both miracle stories and a passion narrative, Fortna concluded that he had identified "a pre-Johannine stratum which had already a distinctive *literary* character imposed upon it."[6] Its author and audience seem to have been bilingual (Greek and Aramaic).[7] It was a missionary tract with a single end, to show (presumably to the potential Jewish convert) that Jesus is the messiah.[8]

Employing certain punctuation marks, Fortna concludes his study by printing out in Greek what was in the source. Parentheses indicate passages that are not certainly to be assigned to it, square brackets enclose conjectural or uncertain readings, and double brackets are placed around passages whose place in the source is uncertain. The siglum | . . . | stands for places where Jn has made insertions into the source. The result is roughly the following (lacking the above indications and not listing parts of verses rather than whole verses where they occur):

Introduction

Exordium **1**:6, 7
The Baptist's testimony **1**:19–21, 23, 26, 27, 33, 32, 34
The conversion of the first disciples **3**:23–24; **1**:35–50
The Signs of Jesus
1. *Water changed into wine* **2**:1–3, 5–11
2. *A nobleman's son healed* **2**:12a; **4**:46b–47, 49–54
3. *A miraculous draught of fish* **21**:2–8b, 10–12, 14
4. *The multitude fed* **6**:1–3, 5, 7–14. *Interlude: walking on water* 15b–22, 25
5. *A dead man raised: a Samaritan woman* **11**:1–4, 7, 11, 15; **4**:4–7, 9, 16–19, 25–26, 28–30, 40, 41; **11**:17–20, 28, 32–34, 38–39, 41–45
6. *A man blind from birth healed* **9**:1–3a, 6–8
7. *A thirty-eight year illness healed* **5**:2–3, 5–9, 14
The Death and Resurrection of Jesus
The cleansing of the temple and death plot **2**:14–16, 18–19; **11**:47a, 53
The anointing of Bethany **12**:1–5, 7–8
The triumphal entry **12**:12–15
The last supper Fragments of the source's account in **12**:27; **13**:(1b), 2a, 4–5, 12–14, 18b, 21b, 26–27, 37–38; **14**:31b; **16**:32b
The arrest (**18**:1–5, 10–12); *Jesus in the high priest's house* (**18**:13, 24, 15–16a, 19–23, 16b–18, 25b–28); *The trial before Pilate* (**18**:28, 33, 37, 38c; **19**:15, **18**:39–40; **19**:6, 12–14a, 1–2, 16); *The crucifixion and burial* (**19**:16–19, 20b, 23–24, 28–29, 30b, 25, 31–34a, 36–38; **3**:1; **19**:39–42)
The resurrection (**20**:1–3, 5, 7–11, 12, 14, 16–20)
Peroration **20**:30–31

If that seems to the casual reader little more than Bultmann's scissors-and-paste rearrangement of the gospel, the impression will be dispelled by a laborious examination of the Greek. That discloses a remarkable consistency of vocabulary and style in the putative source and yields a sequential narrative that is not to be found in the canonical fourth gospel, interrupted as it seems to be by many editorial insertions. The key to Fortna's reconstruction is consistency. He eliminates any interruptions and sudden turns, non-sequiturs, doublets, and passages with dense or overloaded wording.

Fortna's Revisions: The "Predecessor" of the Fourth Gospel

In a book produced almost two decades later, the Vassar College scholar revises his theory in light of the criticisms leveled at it and his own testing of it by the use of slightly altered criteria.[9] This longer and more explicit treatment deserts the Greek in favor of transliteration. It divides the narrative source (SG for "signs gospel") into twenty sections and employs a twofold typographical aid: first, the hypothetical pre-Johannine source printed in boldface and then, in a reversal, the presumed redaction shown in boldface leaving the SG in ordinary type. The latter remains largely as it was in the earlier book. Taking the first chapter as an example, we find Fortna eliminating in his second book phrases and whole verses, leaving a source which opens with the "man . . . whose name was John" giving testimony to Jesus. He has no other role. He is God's agent through whom faith in Jesus is to arise. Jesus is not introduced by name in the SG. He is simply hailed by John as "the Lamb of God," and is identified as the Christ, Elijah, and the prophet by indirection. The climactic christological affirmation is that he is the Son of God. Two disciples of John, Andrew and another unnamed, follow Jesus. Andrew leads Simon to Jesus and Jesus gives him a new name, Cephas. Andrew or Peter, not Jesus, is the "he" who finds the townsman of the two, Philip, in v. 43b. Philip finds Nathanael and calls Jesus the one of whom Moses wrote in the law. (Fortna is unsure whether "and also the prophets" was in the source.) Nathanael hails Jesus as Rabbi, Son of God, and King of Israel.

What must be removed from ch. 1 of the gospel as we have it, after its redaction by the fourth evangelist, in order to arrive at the signs gospel? The following elements: any repetitious or overexplicit details; "the Jews"; Jesus as one unknown, even by John; geographic and time-sequence specificity; theological elaborations, e.g. Jesus as the one who "takes away the sin of the world" and the divinely revealed explanation to John of who he is on whom the dove-Spirit descends; Hebrew words translated into Greek; Nathanael's guilelessness, which is unlike Jacob-Israel's; Jesus' mysterious knowledge, both questioned and explained; and the obviously Johannine "Amen, amen" and "Son of Man," coupled with a second person plural, traditional saying addressed to Nathanael.

A careful breakdown by verses in each of the twenty segments follows both the "pre-Johannine source" (SG) and the "Johannine redaction" (4G). Concluding the segment is a more technical "Analysis" which justifies what has been declared redactional. Here, along with some tight argumentation based on grammar, style and content, phrases proliferate such as "appears to be Johannine" or "little doubt that it stems in some form from the Passion Source." Fortna had given himself at the outset a 7, on a scale of 10, for confidence in his own choices. He also modestly states that he should be happy if more than half of what he proposes is convincing to others.

His major conclusions are as follows: that a pre-Johannine document was employed by the fourth evangelist which presented seven or eight miracle stories as signs of Jesus' messiahship to make clear who Jesus is and for no other purpose; that there was pre-Johannine passion material that accounted for why Jesus the messiah had to die by claiming that "these things happened to fulfill scripture"; that the fact that Jesus worked the signs of the messiah means that the new age has appeared, there being no mention of future expectation in SG; and that, although Jesus does go from Galilee to Judea in SG, there is no interest in region (as distinct from place names) as such, hence all negative reference to *Ioudaioi* ("Judeans" for Fortna) is added by the evangelist because of the harassment Christian Jews were experiencing from Jews more generally in his time and place.

Another Attempt To Recover the Gospel of Signs

Urban C. von Wahlde's attempt to isolate the first version of Jn appeared a year after Fortna's.[11] It bears the regretful note that, as *The Fourth Gospel and Its Predecessor* appeared after von Wahlde's book was in press, he could not discuss it in detail. But he does observe that Fortna sought only to analyze the redactional additions within the signs material, leaving the choices of *The Gospel of Signs* largely intact. Von Wahlde, of Chicago's Loyola University, sets about identifying signs material by applying these criteria: vocabulary or linguistic differences; thought-pattern or ideological differences (thirteen in number); four theological features; five minor characteristics useful in identifying signs material. Applying these to chs. 1—20 of the FG (and having decided that the miracle of 21:1–11 did not stem from the same tradition as the signs material), he arrives at thirty-seven pericopes found in chs. 1—7, 9—12 and 18—20.[12] The longest is of twenty-six verses (ch. 11); eight are of two or three verses only.

Von Wahlde's method does not begin with an examination of the miracle and passion narratives but goes from the aporias disclosing literary seams to the variation in vocabulary ("language") employed for the same realities. He then proceeds to elements of thought within the gospel such as hostility to Jesus ("ideology"), which occur in ways contradictory or inconsistent with each other. Differences in religious thought ("theology") as between a first and second edition provide his third workable criterion. Taking his cue from Wellhausen, Spitta, and more modernly M.C. White,[13] von Wahlde in probing the FG's terms for religious authorities discovers that "Pharisees," "chief priests" and "rulers" occur consistently within one set of pericopes and "Jews" as a hostile term in another. The latter can also mean simply people who are Jews or Jews of the southern province, Judea, but in thirty-seven of its seventy-one occurrences in the gospel it means those Jews set against Jesus.

Concentrating on the passages that feature this usage as contrasted with the other terms for Jewish authorities ("Pharisees," "chief priests," and "rulers," used singly or coupled), von Wahlde then applies his other criteria to the Jews-as-hostile pericopes. In the latter the word *erga* is always used for miracles, but in the three neutral descriptions of authorities, *sēmeia.* "Sign" always has the positive meaning of miracle except in 2:18 and 6:30 (where Jesus is challenged to perform a sign defensively as proof, both times in conjunction with "Jews," 2:18 and 6:41). "Works" is a word for miracles in passages that employ "Jews"; but it also bears the dualistic meaning from apocalyptic writing of doing the will of God or the devil. Jesus describes his ministry as a whole as "work" (4:34; 17:4). Examples of the coupling of "signs" and neutral terms like "ruler of the Jews," "Pharisees," and "chief priests" occur in 3:1–2; 7:31–32; 9:16. Such passages become, for von Wahlde, the building-blocks of the first edition of the FG. Contrariwise, in 5:15 and 10:24–38 "Jews" is used in conjunction with the verb "work" and the noun "works." This twofold correlation of signs/authorities and works/Jews is both consistent and exclusive throughout the gospel. Separate authorship of two strands of writing is concluded to be the key, not "works" on the lips of Jesus only as some had previously thought.[14] The one exception to the works/Jews pattern is 6:26, even though "Jews" does not occur in the passage until vv. 41 and 52. "Jews" refers to the territory of Judea in 3:22 and means Judeans in 3:25 (its sole occurrence in the singular); 11:19, 31, 33, 36, 45, 54; 12:9, 11; 19:20. In these places there is mention of Judea or Jerusalem and no note of hostility attaches to it. More importantly, the occurrences in chs. 11, 12 and 19 are in conjunction with the terms Pharisees, chief priests and rulers.

**Adding Ideology and Theology to Vocabulary
as Criteria for the Signs-Gospel**

Von Wahlde terms this distinct, twofold usage his primary linguistic criterion. A secondary one that "checks out" when applied to passages determined by it or identified by ideological and theological criteria as belonging to the signs source is that words that refer to Jewish religious concepts are first given in Hebrew, then in Greek (1:38, 41, 42; 2:23; 20:16) while place names are generally given first in Greek, then in Hebrew (Aramaic): 5:2; 19:13, 17. An exception is 6:1, which is a juxtaposition rather than a translation. Of the above, only 2:23, 5:2 and 6:1 occur in passages determined by the first or linguistic criterion.

The Earliest Version goes on to uncover ten differences in thought or perspective between the signs material and the remainder of the gospel. These include stereotyped formulas of immediate or easy belief ("and his disciples/many/even of the rulers/the Judeans, believed in him"), emphasis on the number and greatness of the signs, emphasis on the variety of groups that come to believe in Jesus, and the hostility of the Pharisees as something that increases slowly and is marked by unsuccessful action (7:32) and uncertainty (12:19), then a final, decisive move (18:3). There is a division of opinion regarding Jesus in the signs material. In it, too, narrative predominates, punctuated by brief exchanges, but there are no extended discourses. Theologically, belief is based on the performance of signs in this material and it is presented as following easily upon the miracle, even though not all capitulate in faith (see the holding back of some "authorities," the probable "they" of 12:37, while other Sanhedrin members believe (v. 42a). This first or "Jewish-authorities" edition presents belief in Jesus within the categories of a traditional christology such as "from God" (3:2; 9:33), "a prophet" (4:19), "the prophet" (6:14), "messiah" (1:41; 4:25). In the early edition, too, the supernatural knowledge of Jesus functions to bring about belief, as in the cases of Nathanael (1:47–49) and the Samaritan woman (4:16–19, 39). Jesus possesses such knowledge in the second edition but it functions differently: to show his sovereign superiority to all things human (thus, 2:24–25; 6:15, 64; 18:4–9).

If all the usages in the above paragraph characterize the earliest version of the FG, which employs the terms "Pharisees," "chief priests" and "rulers" for the Jewish authorities, the second edition marked by "Jews" in a hostile sense has these features: ethnic Jews fear "the Jews" (7:13; 9:22; 20:19); the "works" that Jesus performs, which he himself has to draw attention to, serve as testimony but have little (5:36) or no (10:32) effect; Jesus' opponents, "the Jews," are bitterly hostile to him from the start, there is no sense of building climax (2:18–22; 5:10–20), even seeking to stone (8:59; 10:31) or to kill him (5:18; 7:1; 11:8); "the Jews" are never divided over Jesus (see 9:18–23) nor are the people described as being divided over him; dialogue and discourse material (2:18–22, 5:10–47; 6:30–59; 7:14–19, 33–36; 8:13–29, 48–59; 10:22–39) largely overtakes narrative; Jesus' "works" become but one of four witnesses to him; a high christology that identifies Jesus with God (5:18; 8:58; 10:33) replaces the traditional messianic titles.

Von Wahlde concludes that, despite the limitations of his enterprise, there is much that can be known of the structure and theology of the signs material. Central to it are the number and power of Jesus' signs, which increase in magnitude (going from the earliest healings to that of the man *born* blind and the raising of Lazarus). The people's belief and the hostility of the authorities grow commensurately. Although christologically God is spoken of as being with Jesus, who is both a prophet and messiah, Jesus performs all the signs by his own authority. The clearest background for the Johannine signs is that of the description in Exodus and Numbers of the signs given to Moses, as the studies of Teeple (1957), Glasson (1963) and Meeks (1967) had already shown. But Moses-typology is not paramount in the signs source. Rather, Jesus is mainly depicted there as the expected one of Israel, its messiah (1:42; 4:25, 29), king (1:49), and Son of God (*ibid.*). As messiah, "no one will know where he comes from" (7:27), yet it cannot be conceived that Jesus has performed fewer signs than the messiah will at his coming (v. 31). Christ or prophet, the signs amply sustain his title to being both. The gospel's christology, judging from what remains to us, focuses almost exclusively on the importance of the miraculous.

From Neutrality to Hostility:
A New Christology in the Second Edition of the SG

There is no polemic against John in the signs source. He is shown simply as one who testified to Jesus, being neither the Christ, Elijah nor the prophet. Unlike Jesus, he "did no sign" (10:41). The signs gospel is Jewish and traditional, written for Jews against a backdrop of their standard view of Moses. It relates details of Jesus' life that we know from no other source, including the affinity of his career with the Baptist movement. It is a document that shows familiarity with numerous locales in Palestine, religious customs, and feasts (Sukkoth, 7:2 and Hanukkah, 10:22, besides Pesaḥ). We cannot accurately construct from it the number of Jesus' trips to Judea but it catalogues his extensive activity there, chiefly in Jerusalem. The signs gospel was proclamational rather than apologetic. It originated in perhaps 70–80 C.E. in "association with the southern part of Palestine."[15] The same community from which it came probably produced the second edition. Of its author nothing can be known from within the reconstructed text.

The second stage of the community's history lets us know about a bitter struggle over exclusion of the Jesus-believing Jews from the synagogue. Von Wahlde assigns 9:18–23, which contains *aposyna-gōgos,* a word of uncertain precision (v. 22), to the middle of the three editions[16] and supposes that it has been added to 12:42 by redaction.[17] This second edition has assigned a symbolism to Jesus' signs different from the reason for their presence in the signs gospel (see 6:26–58, the synagogue instruction on bread at Capernaum; 9:35–41, a spiritual meaning given to blindness and sight; 11:25b–26, a similar interpretation of Lazarus' resuscitation and new life). The redacted version of the first edition speaks of belief as if it has a deeper foundation than simply seeing signs. There are other "witnesses" (a term used in this second edition), but one cannot respond to any of them with belief unless one possesses the Spirit. The Nicodemus episode (3:3–21 added in the second edition to 2:23; 3:1–2 of the signs gospel) makes this clearest of all. Jesus is here calling for a new form of existence. The same is true of the addition of 4:10–15, 20–24, 31–38, 40–42 in the story of the Samaritan woman. Of ch. 7, only 25–27, 31–32, 40–52 are from the signs gospel; the remainder is probably from the second edition but may come from the third, to which von Wahlde assigns the discussion of Jesus' "whence" and "whither": earthly origin/heavenly origin; the diaspora/his return to the Father.

In the first edition the disciples are presented as responding properly to each of the four witnesses of Jesus: to John (1:35–49); to the sign at Cana (2:1–11); to the scriptures (2:13–17, 22); to the word of Jesus (2:18–22). They then largely disappear from the narrative until the last supper. The theology of the second edition, which sees the possession of the Spirit as the basis for all believing response to Jesus, conceives the giving of the Spirit, nonetheless, as taking place only after Jesus is glorified (7:37–39; 20:22). The christology of the second edition probably reaches its peak in 10:22–39. It is there that in response to the query whether he is the messiah he speaks of God as "my Father" and claims to be "God's Son," saying "I and the Father are one" and "the Father is in me and I in him." There, too, he is challenged with "making himself equal to God."

The recovered "earliest version" of the book's title can be read through in sequence in Chapter 3, going from one pericope to the next. Of the thirty-seven in all, eight are in the passion narrative. The one risen-life pericope is the appearance to Mary Magdalene. Setting the various terms for Jewish authorities in boldface ("Jews" only in the meaning "Judeans") identifies the primary criterion of selection. Unlike some other source-sleuths, von Wahlde unhesitatingly assigns connective phrases of time and place to his *source*. He does not claim that the portions of the signs gospel that have survived to the canonical John are its complete form. Neither does he presume to say what editing it may have undergone, only the basic changes it did *not* undergo as it proceeded to a second and a third edition (the Jn that we have). The attentive reader will naturally be on guard to find exceptions that fall outside his generalizations and will examine with care his reasons for assigning passion and risen-life narratives to the signs source.[18] He constantly refers to his differences from Bultmann, Brown, Fortna, Boismard-Lamouille and others who track the FG's sources or redactional stages so that judgments can be made on their respective arguments. If he is right, even in fair measure, then much has been resolved about puzzling sequences, abrupt changes in style and content, and above all the distressing hostility to "the Jews" in the FG. For, like Brown and Fortna, von Wahlde ascribes its bitter tone to an editing that came after the grave harassment and even ejection of the Jesus-believing Jews from ordinary Jewish life— somewhere in Palestine, he would say.

The Contributions of Smith, Martyn and Lindars

D. Moody Smith is, in a sense, the dean of U.S. Johannine specialists, as much through the dissertations he has directed and the teaching careers he has launched as through his articles and scholarly lectures. He published a collection of his writings produced between 1961 and 1981, for which he wrote an introductory essay, "Johannine Christianity."[19] After reviewing the results of various modes of analysis of the FG like the redaction-critical,[20] he identifies the greater part of the discourse or sayings material as forming the basis for what is truly Johannine. By this he means the work of the evangelist who preceded the final redactor. For Smith 1 Jn has the same "distinctively Johannine ring." It is but a short step from the Paraclete passages of 14:25–26 and 16:12–15 "to the conjecture that the words of Jesus in the Fourth Gospel, so obviously spoken from the standpoint of a spirit-inspired post-resurrection community (cf. John 7:39; 20:22), are to be regarded as the fulfillment of the promise of the Paraclete rather than the words of the historical Jesus."[21]

Smith notes his agreement in principle with the identification of an independent Johannine narrative tradition, if not Fortna's gospel of signs, and points to mounting evidence for the existence of a Johannine discourse tradition as well.[22] He remains in an older mold of Jn scholarship with his statement that the miracle tradition may embody a *theios anēr*[23] christology from a pre-gospel collection that may be called an aretalogy. The same can be said of his judgment that "it . . . does not seem possible to explain the entire history of the Johannine tradition against such a background [Judaism and the outlook of Christian Jews]."[24] Yet twenty years before he had reported "a loose, but real, consensus" on the fundamentally semitic and even Jewish character of the Johannine tradition and preaching.[25] Smith is at ease distinguishing between a cycle of miracle stories existing independently from a passion narrative, the former probably originating among those who had been disciples of the Baptist and directed to this sect to get them to change allegiance, the latter to convince Jews generally that Jesus was the messiah, as a signs-source alone would not have succeeded in doing.[26]

Raymond E. Brown refers to a "strong current movement rejecting a proposed pre-Johannine Signs-source gospel"[27] in reviewing a recent dissertation from the University of Basel.[28] The author, W.J. Bittner, examines the term *sēmeion* at length, prompted by its non-use in the synoptic tradition. He attributes Jn's peculiar positive use of it, not to that gospel's drawing on a prophet-like-Moses theme, but on the strongly Davidic Isaiah 11. This Isaian background of the usage of Jn, who employs signs positively to elicit faith in Jesus as Christ and Son of God, is Bittner's main thesis.

J. Louis Martyn wrote a very influential book in the period just before our starting date of 1970 but revised it in a second edition well into that decade.[29] In it he concluded that Jn 9 (and 5 and 7 like it) was a two-level drama constructed by the evangelist in which the man born blind was a Jew of Jerusalem who was also made to represent those Jewish members of the separated church in an unidentified diaspora city. Its messianic faith in Jesus, as a result of his miracles, led to their ejection from the synagogue. Martyn understands this as a formal excommunication resulting from the "awesome [twelfth] Benediction" of the *Shemone Esre* (Eighteen) which declared *minim*—a word he translates "heretics"—to be accursed. In his reconstruction, the academy at Iavneh under Gamaliel II had inserted that curse sometime around 85 and it was being used to catch believers in Jesus as messiah. Since no previous Jewish writing had said that the messiah would be a wonder-worker, Jesus could have been no more than a magician, a deceiver, or so the emerging rabbinate thought. He was accused of leading people astray (Jn 7:12, 47), a charge that Martyn takes to mean entice (*yasāth*) them to believe in more than one God. A passage from the Mishnah of ca. 180 (*Sanhedrin* 7, 10–11) lumps together *enticing* to idolatry with the promise of wonders, *leading astray* (see Deut 13:2–3, 6), and *practicing sorcery* or magic, as deeds deserving death. The accusation on such charges was being made against believers in Jesus as the result of a rabbinic decree that went out to diaspora synagogues as early as the writing of Jn. A *baraita* (= "outside" the Mishnah) of the period 200–400, describing the hanging and stoning of Yeshu on the eve of the Passover on the above three charges, is also presented as evidence (*Sanhedrin* 43a). The Johannine community, knowing that the performance of signs was no part of messianic expectation, had apparently been casting Jesus in the mold of the prophet like Moses (Deut 18:15) who gave bread from the heavens. It did not save them, however, from harassment unto death for claiming they knew the messiah to be a crucified wonder-wonder, for the terms were wrong.

In a paper presented in 1975 Martyn continued to be convinced that the curse on a Jew who had a soft policy on God's oneness (a *min*) corresponded to that person's becoming or being declared *aposynágōgos* (Jn 9:22; 12:42; 16:2).[30] This "highly probable correspondence" becomes within the same paragraph a "*Festpunkt*" (fixed or basing point). Following from it, the argument is presented that underlying Jn 1:35–40 is a homily directed to Jews of the kind meant by Paul when he spoke of a "gospel of the circumcision" (Gal 2:7). Someone, probably the evangelist John, had edited it awkwardly to make Jesus take the initiative in calling Philip (v. 43) as he does with the apostles in the other synoptics. The early homilist, however, had portrayed men who *came* (vv. 39, 46, 47) to Jesus and *found* (vv. 41, 45) him to be the messiah. In the same way, the preacher hoped that many hearers would come and find Jesus.

The early period represented by this pericope before its editing was marked by much success. Jews were preaching Jesus to Jews in a synagogue framework and many came to believe in him (see 2:11; 4:53; 6:14). The group of believers "experienced no social dislocation and felt relatively little alienation from their heritage."[31] The middle period followed upon excommunication from the synagogue and some martyrdoms, making the group into a separate community. The Logos hymn is probably to be assigned to this period. As Martyn paraphrases the situation, "The Messiah came to his own world,/ and his own people did *not* receive him."[32] The late period witnessed further homilies but also the climactic writing of the full Johannine gospel in its first and second editions. In this matter Martyn concurs with his Union Theological Seminary colleague Brown in his five-stage analysis. The authorities had evidently laid down the dictum in the middle period, Jesus or Moses, and believers in Jesus had opted for him as their (late period, Greek-designated) "Christ." The "Jewish Christians" have thus come into existence; "Christian Jews" remain undeclared, in the synagogues. The "other sheep not of this fold" are the latter group, who are "of the world" (see 8:31ff., 12:42).

Barnabas Lindars authored a commentary on Jn in the New Century Bible,[33] at the conclusion of which he delivered four lectures, published earlier, containing some of the ideas expressed in it.[34] These ideas on Johannine traditions he continued to hold in his Leuven lecture at the same conference as Martyn's above.[35] In agreement with Brown (on pp. XXXIV–LI), as Lindars puts it, he assumes that "the gospel is based on the evangelist's own sermons, which he has united to form the complete book."[36] Despite the temporal aporias, the thematic breaks, and the recurring pattern of signs (each of them constituting an epiphany of the divine man)—all of which Lindars acknowledges—there is a *prima facie* case for supposing that Jn "began life as separate homilies, which the evangelist subsequently used as the basis for a continuous Gospel. The discourse, then, is not a report of an actual debate. . . . It is rather a sermon addressed to the Christians in order to deepen and strengthen their faith in a situation where Jewish objections to Christianity [*sic*] are a matter of vital concern."[37]

Oscar Cullmann's *The Johannine Circle* suggests the following process of composition; the author, a strong personality, called on common traditions and others special to him, not excluding personal reminiscences, producing the main lines of the work as we have it now. A circle of redactors or a single one revised or completed the whole work after his death, most likely in Syria or Transjordania.[38] We shall be returning to this book below (pp. 45f.) to see what Cullmann thinks about Samaritans in the Jn community.

A "Priority" That Does Not Mean First To Be Composed

Before leaving the question of sources of the FG a report must be filed on that work of the last decade that denied most vehemently that John, son of Zebedee (who wrote Jn), drew on any sources. It is Bishop John A.T. Robinson's *The Priority of John,* in effect a detailed discussion of the entire gospel. The book does *not* hold as its main thesis what the title might suggest, namely that Jn was composed *in toto* before the other three.[39] Robinson's considerably more nuanced position is that his title "does not necessarily mean the temporal priority of John" but the case for a "procedural" priority—a complete openness to such temporal priority, to be sure, "though I should be inclined to think that the writing that went into the Fourth Gospel may well have begun earlier *and* gone on later than in the case of the others."[40] That sentence is the tip-off to the amount of openness the bishop is willing to allow. He does not wish to deal with one formal interdependence among the four gospels, i.e. the literary. That, he rightly describes as a problem that no longer looms large in scholarly perspective. But the interrelatedness of the four gospels is something he thinks will not go away.

He opts for the position that Jn was "a primary source in whose light they too [the synoptics] can be viewed."[41] This is put forward as a hypothesis, a means of exploring what happens if one reverses the prevailing assumption that Jn is not a primary source. As to source criticism of the fourth gospel, Robinson has a poor opinion of it. He seems happy to quote an opinion of Kysar on the contents of the signs source/gospel as proposed by Teeple, Fortna (*TGOS*), Nicol, Schnackenburg and Jürgen Becker, that "source criticism is 'somewhat in shambles'."[42] No matter that Kysar had limited his observation to method in source criticism. For Robinson the outcome is in no better condition than the method employed.

He engages in a book-length polemic against the idea that the FG "is so remote in time from the situation it describes that it could not credibly in any sense be a first Gospel."[43] The bishop sees no reason to depart in this, the last book of his life, from his earlier proposed chronology of the composition of Jn spelled out in *Redating the New Testament*.[44] There he had argued for the following rough stages:

30–50	Shaping of the Gospel material in dialogue with Palestinian Judaism
50–55	Preaching in the Ephesus area and the first edition of the Gospel
60–65	The Epistles, responding to the challenges of false teachers
65+	Second edition of the Gospel with Prologue and Epilogue[45]

Historical Happenings, Not Documents, As Jn's Source

It seems quite unproven to Robinson that John depended on sources. The FG for him gives no indication of standing in an external and second-hand relation to other elements of a tradition that its author took over, making use of it and working on it. At the heart of his argumentation is the question of historicity. He grants that this is independent of the matter of establishing sources, but it is "certainly not irrelevant to the question of whether John goes back to source rather than sources."[46] The interrelation of tradition and event, however complex it may be, is not so simple as to say that the question of that relation can only be raised after the literary task of separating redaction from tradition is complete.[47] "The presumption is surely justified that an underlying event has at some point controlled the reports rather than simply the reports each other."[48] Thus, the historicity of Nicodemus and of Martha and Mary of Bethany is much better accounted for by the fact that there were such persons to whom such things happened—divergent descriptions being a common event—than that (in the latter case) John and Luke were using each other or some underlying source. Robinson maintains in the same discussion that there are "basically three *independent* traditions of the trial and death of Jesus, the Markan, the Lukan and the Johannine, and that each goes back, directly or indirectly to source."[49] "Source" is what happened in history retained in different traditional tellings, as is the case with reports on events in life generally. History never quite puts us in touch with the facts, he makes clear, but with somebody's (or somebody else's) version of the facts (in a quotation from A.H.N. Green-Armytage of 1952). If this seems a cavalier dismissal of the immensely complex problem of gospel composition, Robinson challenges the reader to cope with his forest of arguments in favor of gospel events' having happened as described. The Johannine version is presented as being at least as trustworthy historically as any other, and without demonstrable dependence on a synoptic account.

The gospel according to John is a primary source. That is Robinson's first, last and foremost contention. It is "at any rate *a* first written statement of the gospel, of primal rather than secondary significance."[50] He thinks "in fact that all the gospels were coming into being over a period more or less simultaneously, and at different stages their traditions and their redaction could well show signs of mutual influence—as well as, of course, among the Synoptists, of common written sources."[51] This is a way of acknowledging the validity of the great body of gospel scholarship with which Robinson is familiar while holding fast to the priority of John. The latter means "begin[ning] with what John has to tell us on its own merits and ask[ing] how the others fit, historically and theologically, into that, are illumined by it, and in turn illumine it."[52] The best of all scholarly worlds is not repudiated by such a claim, even as the claimant holds fast to his basic conviction: no sources behind John except what happened, as John successively interpreted these happenings.

In an even-handed estimate of Robinson's performance— something he did not always receive from his critics in life—D. Moody Smith points out correctly that he is more at pains to make the case for Jn's independence and historicity than its priority.[53] In the matter of that second concern, many of his historical-critical judgments are deemed "plausible or possible (e.g., [his] affirmation of John's two-year ministry and passion chronology against the Synoptics). Few, if any, are fantastic." Yet Smith underscores that Robinson is always the controversialist and advocate, never the neutral arbiter of the data.

One needs to be clear before tackling this large and somewhat undisciplined book if one wants to follow the author in his determination that everything in Jn can be shown to go back to source (meaning Jesus) rather than to intermediate traditional sources. Bishop Robinson had prepared a draft of eight chapters for the Bampton Lectures series, which C.F.D. Moule then delivered as Robinson was dying. A sterner hand by the editor, J.F. Coakley, would have made it a better book, but he may have thought he had no such mandate with regard to the final testament of this champion of the British tradition in biblical scholarship.

"Circle" or "School"? Cullmann and Culpepper

The real importance of Cullmann's *The Johannine Circle* cited above probably lies in its contention that ch. 4 tell us much about the outreach of Hellenistic missionaries to Samaria. The exchange by Jacob's well was "an event in the life of Jesus and at the same time [an indication of] its extension in the work performed by the exalted Christ in his church."[54] Luke in Acts 8 reports on a mission to the town of Samaria led by the Greek-speaking Jew Philip (6:5) which, despite the Simon incident, was marked by considerable success (see 8:8, 25). Cullmann thinks that the evangelization of Samaria had to transcend the thorny question of the correct site for worship, as its sanctuary on Mount Gerizim might still have been in use. By putting the prophecy of a future mission to Samaria on Jesus' lips in a conversation with a Samaritan woman, Jn may be legitimizing it in circles where it is disputed ("Do not go into the cities of Samaria," Mt 10:5). Jesus planted the seed. ("They [the people of Sychar] left the town and came to him," 4:30.) The true harvest would be gathered only after his death. In Cullmann's reconstruction, vv. 37b–38 say:

"One sows, another reaps."[55]
I sent you to reap
what you had not worked for.
Others [than Jesus, viz., the Hellenists of Ac 6—8] have
     done the labor,
and you [Peter and John, for the Jerusalem church, Ac 8:14]
     have come into their gain

Cullmann says he was the first to call attention to the link between the Hellenists of Acts—the Stephen party—and Jn.[56] His theory is that Jn is crediting Greek-speaking ethnic Jews of a heterodox bent (his term) as the true missionaries of Samaria, not the Jerusalem apostles, which is the tendency of Acts.

Doctoral dissertations can enshrine important research, usually on a topic that has not previously been isolated or examined with such care. Alan Culpepper working under Moody Smith at Duke University decided that the scholarly world had been using the term "the school of John" without precision ever since Renan first coined it a century and a quarter ago, and he wondered if the usage was valid. He examined nine circles of study from the ancient world to which the term "school" has been applied or, by the criteria that emerged, can be.[57] Five represent pagan learning and four Jewish: the Pythagorean school, the Academy (Plato), the Lyceum (Aristotle), the Garden (Epicurus), the Stoa (Zeno), the school at Qumrân (the righteous teacher), the house of Hillel, Philo's school (a deduction), and the school of Jesus. Most of the schools examined shared nine characteristics.[58] Applied to the gospel and the epistles of John, but without taking Revelation into account or adopting a firm stand on authorship, Culpepper concluded it was right to speak of a Johannine "school" on the model of the others.

Its characteristics were the following.[59] (1) It was a "fellowship" of "disciples" ("brothers," "friends"), first of Jesus, then students taught about Jesus by the "beloved disciple." (2) This BD led and guided the Johannine community, going back to its beginnings. (3) The founder's traditions and teachings were reckoned the true interpretations of the words and deeds of Jesus and the meaning of the scriptures; as collected by the evangelist they could be called a "writing." (4) Members of the community were disciples or students of the founder, the BD (see "we," 21:24). (5) Teaching, learning, studying (the scriptures), and writing were common activities in the community, which (6) observed a communal meal, and had (7) rules or practices regulating admission and retention of membership. (8) The community kept some distance from society ("the world") in a progressive withdrawal (1 Jn 2:19; and see Jn 15:18; 16:2; 17:9). (9) It also developed organizational means of ensuring its perpetuity, from the death of the BD onward. Culpepper's most arguable conclusion is that the BD, who was not the evangelist, as he assumes 19:34b–35 establishes, has by analogy the same relation to Jesus that Jesus had to the Father (3:35; 15:9). More than this, he fulfilled the role in the community that the gospel's Paraclete-sayings predict the Paraclete would. "Just as Jesus had been the first Paraclete for the original group of disciples, so the BD had been the first Paraclete for the Johannine community. . . . After the BD died, it was necessary to affirm that the BD was not . . . the only Paraclete, but that the Paraclete was Spirit (14:26) and that he would remain always (14:17)."[60] The evangelist thus combined, apparently for the first time, the concepts of Paraclete and Spirit, reassuring the community that although their Paraclete, the BD, had died, the work of the Paraclete would continue.

The Who, Where and Why of the Gospel and the Letters

The last word in this chapter should go to Martin Hengel, if only because his *The Johannine Question* gives the impression that it is the last word. What is the Johannine question?[61] It is: Who wrote the gospel and the letters, where, and why? The answer? John the elder, who was the head of a school in Asia Minor between 60/70 and 100/110. He had gone there from Palestine to flee the Jewish War, perhaps came from a family of priestly aristocrats, was in contact with Jesus as his disciple as a young man, and lived to a great age. He could not have been John the son of Zebedee who was the second in the earliest community after Peter, but he did model himself after that "disciple whom Jesus loved" and later fused the image of that John with his own.[62] "How far the specific 'beloved disciple' passages go back wholly to him and how far they are partially shaped by the redactional work of the editor(s) is hard to decide."[63] There was, in any case, an idealization of the son of Zebedee by John the elder, whose pupils impressed on the enigmatic figure of the BD *their* teacher.

The school at Ephesus founded by this impressive "disciple of the Lord" (so Papias) could have produced the Apocalypse after the Neronian persecution and reworked it early in the reign of Trajan. The gospel grew slowly. Because it was directed against the Petrine-synoptic tradition it was published toward the end of the elder's life, with ch. 17 added later and the prologue last. We cannot tell its stages or the author's literary sources, but the whole is a literary unit (Ruckstuhl and Schweizer are right against Bultmann, Richter and Fortna). The alterations and corrections were constant and his pupils left his inconsistencies in place, "perhaps . . . even . . . as a provocation!"[64] In part this was because the ongoing teaching was oral and the gospel was but a testamentary by-product left late in life. Some of the elder's former pupils created a crisis by finding the christology of the school untenable in light of the divine immutability and impassibility. Their secession elicited the three letters and such portions of the gospel as the prologue, chs. 6 and 10, and passages in the farewell discourses.[65]

The scholarship reflected in Hengel's eighty-five pages of notes is a treasure trove, whatever one may think of the conclusions he comes to. Especially important in his marshaling of the second century evidence on Johannine authorship and on the non-espousal of Jn by any gnostic group except the Valentinian Christians. The problematical "synod of Jamnia" and the even more doubtful expulsion of Christians from the synagogue via the Eighteen Benedictions is well dealt with in a discussion of Jewish persecution of Christians, especially in Asia Minor.[66]

3
John as Religious Literature

It is possible to catch glimpses of the history of the Johannine community (or of late first century life in a corner of the empire) through the window of John's gospel, but the evangelist's writing is not primarily history, it is a story. It tells the story of a man and what happened to him, what he said and what he did, whom he related to and how he ended—and will never end. Because Jesus is believed in by many with religious faith as godhead in humanity, there has always been a certain hesitation to view the gospel stories as stories. They have been praised for their narrative power but more often viewed as repositories of revealed doctrine. Because the *genre* of history was so much to the fore in the years around 1800, asking whether or not a thing happened as described, the most serious New Testament study of the last two centuries has been historical. Only lately has it become literary in any sense other than the tracking of sources. Sometimes expositors of the Bible use the phrase "critical-historical" but that is a tautology. Until now the one has meant the other—at least in biblical study.

But an art critic is not an historian. Neither is a literary critic. Both exercise their critical faculties by describing how art objects speak to them, to people of refined taste, to people generally. The literary critic is shocked to learn that literary criticism means, to the Bible scholar, approaching "a text with, so to say, a dissecting knife in his hand, looking out particularly for breaks in continuity . . . for disturbing duplications . . . and for variations in the use of language in different parts of the text, all of them leading to, not appreciation of its merit, but a determination of sources."[1] It must be admitted, conversely, that literary critics have shied away from practicing their art on biblical narratives apart from attention to a few lively tales like the encounter between David and Goliath. Sacred and profane have long inhabited different worlds, even when the two are engaged in the same enterprise. Petersen and Rhoads are two U.S. scholars who broke the silence with their studies of Mark as a narrative, employing the rhetorical analysis of Czech, Russian, British, and American students of the story-teller's art.[2] Rhoads collaborated with a colleague in literary studies. Meanwhile, Frank Kermode in England and Northrop Frye in Canada, neither one trained in the Bible, produced works of criticism on biblical material, Kermode on Mark's gospel in particular.[3]

The Beginnings of a Genuine Literary Criticism of Jn: Culpepper

A few essays on Johannine irony and symbolism had preceded David W. Wead's Basel dissertation on Jn's literary techniques[4] but it remained for Alan Culpepper to produce a thorough exploration of Jn as literary art.[5] The historically oriented New Testament scholars already had a term to describe it, "composition criticism," meaning an evangelist's work as author rather than editor. But they did not have in mind the highly developed art of narrative criticism, of the existence of which they were barely aware. Culpepper dove deeply into the literary critical studies of such well-regarded figures as Booth, Chatman, Genette, Scholes and Kellogg, Sternberg, and Uspensky. He asked "What are they saying about narrative?" to learn what this writing might have to say about Jn. Like those who had analyzed Mk before him (and Kingsbury, Mt after him),[6] Culpepper methodically explored the following categories as they applied to Jn: narrator and point of view, narrative time, plot, characters, implicit commentary, and the implied reader.

Carefully examining Jn's twenty-one chapters under these aspects, Culpepper found its first hearers invited to enter a literary world created by the author from materials drawn from life and history, imagination and reflection. Jn "speaks retrospectively, telling a story that is a sublime blend of historical tradition and faith."[7] In this story the narrator (the voice Jn assumes in telling the story), shares the point of view of the actual author (who in taking on the role of author is called "the implied author"). He is as if omni-scient and hence is not a character in the story; he breaks in on it throughout with helpful explanations and reminders; and he is entirely reliable in his judgments on persons and events. The hearer is thus inclined from the outset to adopt the narrator's view of Jesus and the response of others to him. The narrator does this by situating the story's place in history between "the beginning" (1:1) and "the last day" (6:40). He is also fully aware of the "whence" and "whither" of Jesus (6:46; 13:36; 16:5) as one who comes forth as word-in-flesh from the bosom of the Father, and has gone back to the one who has sent him. The characters in the gospel are sharply defined by "their response to Jesus, by the measure of their ability to believe, and by their progress toward or away from the perspective of the narrator."[8]

Some reject him, others refuse to confess their faith openly, a few are caught between Jesus and his opponents and must choose whom to follow. The disciples, who react to his "glory" with belief, represent a variety of perceptions of Jesus which must be over-come. Only "the disciple whom Jesus loved" (Culpepper is silent on Jesus' mother in 2:5) is portrayed as responding with belief and love from the first we hear of him (13:23). He is the true witness to Jesus, the model of authentic faith. To hear this gospel with its characters' various reactions to Jesus is not only to enter its narra-tive world but to be moved to consider one's own response. The narrator has an ideal and employs the BD to dramatize it. His message is: overcome as he did whatever lack of understanding of Jesus you have and Jesus will be able to call you, too, disciple and friend; let my ironies get to you as they successively unmask the folly of disbelief and misperception.

The Beloved Disciple as Literary Image of the Narrator

Those to whom this gospel was first directed must have felt the beliefs they held dear clarified and reaffirmed by it. A few were doubtless disconfirmed and angered by the narrator, identi-fied by Culpepper as, in some sense, the beloved disciple. The gospel must have sustained them as they experienced themselves a part of the "we" who had beheld Jesus' glory. Little of that impact has been lost with the centuries, as the cumulative effect of the gospel's rich and powerful narrative is felt by hearers in every age. Plot development is rather loose in this gospel; the rapid progression from scene to scene is best described as episodic. But the FG has a unity and coherence that comes with the way it develops its few themes. The subtle elements of its narrative structure prove more powerful than the obvious ones. At the end, the evangelist's literary world sufficiently touches the real world of many readers that "they can accept his vision of the world as the true, the authentic (*alēthinos*) one."⁹

Erich Auerbach is quoted as saying on an early page in his *Mimesis*, "The world of the Scripture stories is not satisfied with claiming to be a historically true reality—it insists that it is the only real world." As long as any contemporary, post-enlightenment readers insist on seeing in Jn a window on the ancient world, telling exactly what happened during Jesus' ministry, they can never see truth in it. Only when the FG is used as a mirror held up to readers' lives, as the narrator intended, can there be interaction with the glory of Jesus it discloses. This book has to be read or heard as literature because, like everything in the Bible, it *is* literature. It is art and history, it is fiction and truth, all reconciled in the evangelist's deft performance. If these are reconciled *in* the hearers' lives and *with* their lives, Jn can speak to them.

Culpepper says it is no part of his purpose to clarify Jn's composition history. In its present form it is a unity, a literary whole. Its deliberate construction of credibility through appeal to tradition, eyewitness testimony, inspiration (the Paraclete), the authority of an esteemed figure (the BD), and the multiplication of geographic and historical detail cumulatively confirm the claims the narrative makes for itself.¹⁰ Controversy over Jn's distinctive christology was probably the chief reason the author sought credibility. This effort further suggests that one of the major purposes of the FG was to present a corrective view of Jesus.

The narrator from his retrospective stance combines scripture with memory but also uses the historic present tense to convey immediacy—to provide a supremely authoritative interpretation of Jesus' words. Using Jesus' repeated references to his origin and destiny in his farewell speech, the author presents his significance for the author's own time. Indeed, key terms in that discourse like "hour," "glorify," "spirit" and "out of the synagogue" are introduced in early chapters as a way to link up the entire gospel with Jesus' death. "What Jesus says, and the gospel as a whole, represents a massive, daring re-interpretation of Jesus,"[11] always from the life situation of the Johannine community.

Unlike Schnackenburg and von Wahlde, Culpepper thinks it is impossible to tell when Jesus or John the Baptist stops speaking in chapter 3 and when or if the narrator speaks (3:13–21 or 16–21 and 3:31–36).[12] That for him is not a matter of great consequence, since all three reflect the author's speech patterns and point of view.

The closest Culpepper comes to discussing Jn's composition history is to say that an examination of 19:35 and 21:24–25 may throw some light on it.[13] There are probably three persons involved: the implied author, the BD, and the narrator. Using the common technique of story-tellers known as framing, the narrator employs the convention "we" in 1:14, 16 and again at 21:24, addressing the hearers directly in what is generally taken to be the original conclusion of the gospel: "to help you believe . . . that you may have life in his name" (20:31). But another commonly used device employed to give the sense of an ending is the death of the person representing the dominant authorial point of view. Thus, there is 21:23, where the BD's death is implied. This yields a narrator (in another vocabulary, the final redactor) who has idealized an historical figure as the "disciple whom Jesus loved," making him in fact the implied author, i.e. the literary image of the real person who did the writing, a second or superior self. This is the one who knows Jesus intimately and can interpret him reliably. His witness, in a word, is true (1935; 21:24). This solution transcends the historical question of who contributed what to the final text by discovering from the text itself the narrator's view of the literary process.

Culpepper's chapter on plot development in Jn with its application of the central features' sequence, causality, unity, and affective power of the narrative takes the reader deeply into the text. Jesus is first introduced as the revealer of the Father (1:18) and authorizer of the children of God (v. 12), who then slowly "achieves his goals while his fortune apparently changes for the worse."[14] The plot develops as Jesus' identity comes to be recognized and fails to gain recognition. The suspense is provided by the question: Will successive characters in the gospel acknowledge him for who he is and thereby receive eternal life? The same story is repeated over and over. The discourses slow the action down yet provide interpretive interludes that shed light on it. Chapter 12 is the bridge from the successive recognitions or rejections of Jesus to his capture. Following it he experiences the agony of accepting his death (vv. 27–28), through which the name of the Father will be glorified and he will draw us to himself (vv. 27–32). The characters Nicodemus, the disciples, the various beneficiaries of Jesus' signs, and Pilate are the subject of one of Culpepper's chapters, the commentary implicit in the use of misunderstanding, irony and conscious symbolism, of another. His study ends by convincing the reader that the FG is a sophisticated example of the narrative art. As to its authorial audience or intended readership, believers in Jesus seem clearly to be the targeted group rather than Jews who do not believe in him or Samaritans or Gentiles. The believers are expected to know most of the story characters and its general outlines but not about the BD, Lazarus, Nicodemus, or Annas and Caiaphas. A familiarity with Jewish festivals is assumed—not, however, specific places in the land of Israel or Jewish customs. A broader readership was evidently envisioned at a later stage than the one originally intended. As to the overall purpose of the gospel, it has to be authentic faith in Jesus, the revealer of God, as contrasted with inauthentic faith.

Studies in the Johannine Irony

One expansion and elaboration of an aspect of Culpepper's literary inquiry, namely Jn's use of irony, has been provided by his student Paul D. Duke.[15] Duke understands *irony* to be a Hellenistic technique employed to treat themes of primarily Jewish concern. In it, a subtle literary choice is being offered to the first hearers of Jn. The choice is between the surface level of meaning and an alternative level. This sound alternative always provides a higher estimation of Jesus than the one that appears on the surface.

It is, in a word, christological. "The numerous ironic silences of the Gospel and its rich suggestiveness of language seem to presuppose an audience at least partially conditioned to this mode of expression."[12] In Duke's view the technique is less a product of Jewish writings (Esther, Tobit) than of the fifth century Greek tragedies of Sophocles and Euripides as presaged by Homer. The devices basic to Jn's thought assume a bi-level, literary vision, a duality that invites the hearer from one level of comprehension to another. Among the devices are metaphor, double meaning, misunderstanding, and ironic speech proper.

Metaphor is easy to recognize if not always to understand: e.g. the "I AM" sayings, "living water," Jesus' going where he cannot the found, the "grain of wheat [that must] die." The two levels of meaning are deeply identified. In metaphor they invite extension, connection and exploration, whereas in irony they are in opposition. The Johannine double meanings, for their part, convey deliberate ambiguity: one reality is used figuratively to illumine another. Among them are "going up [to the feast]," 7:8; "from above," a better rendering of *anōthen* than "anew," 3:3, 7; "it is expedient for you," 11:50, and "it is to your advantage," 16:7, the same Greek verb; "to die for," 11:50–51; 18:14; "to lift/be lifted up," 3:14; 8:28; 12:32, 34; and "it is finished/completed," 19:30. In every case—and there are others besides these—speakers say more than they realize or else the narrator hints at or leaves open the possibility of a higher level of meaning. The Johannine misunderstandings are well known: those of Nicodemus, the Samaritan woman, the crowd that experienced the miracle of the loaves, the disciples who took Lazarus' "sleep" for death, and Martha who confused resurrection on the last day with the "life" Jesus came to give. In all such cases, those who hear the FG are summoned to a stance superior to that of the characters and are thereby drawn into a circle of enlightenment.

As to the ironies of the gospel properly so called, they are any patterns of speech that imply or assume an intimacy between the author and at least a portion of the audience. This bond conveys to the hearer how to interpret what follows. Sometimes Johannine irony is used as a weapon in controversy, the victims being any persons who presume to have more knowledge ("the Jews"), more privilege (Peter), or more power (Pilate) than they do. Outstanding examples are false claims to know Jesus' origins (6:42; 7:27; 41b–42, 52b) and unconscious testimonies to him (11:48; 12:19; 18:33, 39). But whether used as mockery, witness, or inspiration, Jn's irony offers "constant silent invitations [intended] to persuade believers to become Christians [François Vouga]."[16]

Gail O'Day in a follow-up literary study observes that Bultmann was concerned with the mere fact that Jesus was the revealer of God (*kērygma*) and Käsemann overmuch with the content or *what* of his revelation (*dogma*). She proceeds to show that the *how* of Jesus' revelation is of primary importance to Jn.[17] That accounts for the subtitle of her study, since for her the FG makes its theological claims through the way it tells its story. She too thinks that irony in Jn, which she defines after Muecke as "some form of perceptible contradiction, disparity, incongruity or anomaly,"[18] supplies the key. In support of her contention she analyzes Jn 4:4–42 at greatest length. There she discovers that Jn's principal means of engaging the reader in the Jacob's well story is irony. The chapter employs contrasts and disparities showing two narrative levels, often occurring simultaneously, that are at odds. Repetition also occurs in which the words of one character are picked up and used by another to give them new meaning (e.g. "give me a drink"; v. 7; "give me this water," v. 15). There are ironic contrasts between what is anticipated and what is said (vv. 17 and 18). The opaqueness of the woman or the disciples as to what is going on indicates to hearers that they should do more or other than the characters do, even though these be disciples or favored persons like the woman to whom a revelation is made. In brief, O'Day's point is that, as to proclamation or content, ch. 4 does not advance the hearers' knowledge over what they have been told in the prologue. Only the *narrative mode* through which a *theological claim* is made, both in this chapter and throughout, shows the glory of God revealed in the person of Jesus. Everything in the FG leads to the cross through "a total register . . . of narrative possibilities [:] images, metaphors, and stories."[19] Amos Wilder is further quoted as saying: "We will not behold his glory, glory as of the only Son of the Father," (1:14) until we "allow the Fourth Gospel's narrative embodiment of Jesus have its full say."[20]

**The Passion Story as Part of the Whole Gospel:
A Human Jesus Crucified**

Chapters 18—20 are just as important to the plot of John's gospel for G.D. Nicholson as for O'Day. Both hold this in opposition to Käsemann, who thinks the gospel effectively over when Jesus reports back to the Father in ch. 17.[21] The New Zealand scholar examines the three "lifting up" sayings of Jn (3:14; 8:28; 12:32ff.) in the total context of its ascent/decent or above/below motif and discovers that the crucifixion section is no "mere postscript" (Käsemann). It was not the gospel tradition of a passion narrative, already in place, that required John to do likewise. A crucifixion account was essential to his plot. In it Jesus came to "his own," becoming there a stranger to all but a few who believed in him and understood that he had to return above. The community "beheld his glory" (1:14) through understanding the death of Jesus in the context of his movement back to the Father. The meaning of the events of the passion is withheld from them until they receive the message of his need to ascend (20:17). Only then do they receive the Spirit from the risen Jesus (vv. 19–23). The point Jn makes of the passion narrative is that the crucifixion is not an ignominious death but a return to glory. Nicholson thinks that the reality of the human nature of the earthly Jesus, now glorified, "is not discussed . . . because it was not an issue" for John or his community.[22] It is a major issue for Käsemann, however, who holds that Jn's christology of glory is "naively docetic" because his Jesus is always on the side of God. He is never portrayed as a real, suffering, finite human being.

Marianne Meye Thompson methodically takes Käsemann on and all besides who held this view before him (Baur, Wrede, Wetter, Hirsch). Her study is called *The Humanity of Jesus in the Fourth Gospel*.[23] She is likewise convinced that Bultmann is wrong, who understands Jesus' humanity (*sarx*)—the polar opposite of his divinity that hides the latter from view—to be not an anti-docetic device but a paradox, an offense, that must be overcome by faith. Luise Schottroff is thought to be equally wrong in holding that although Jesus was fully human this fact is irrelevant for faith. Schottroff thinks the FG denies that *any* material reality is relevant, not only the flesh of the revealer, for "the flesh profits nothing" (6:63). Thompson's response to all three is an exhaustive scrutiny of Jesus' human origins, the materiality of his signs, and the death of Jesus in Jn. She finds this gospel neither docetic nor anti-docetic. Jn affirmed Jesus' divine identity in the strongest possible terms, but for him that did not obliterate his humanity. His human status "does not finally limit or *define* him; nevertheless, his uniqueness or *un*likeness does not efface his humanity."[24]

Initial Explorations of the Sociological Setting of Jn

David Rensberger in his *Johannine Faith and Liberating Community*[25] joins the many who think that a particularly powerful theologian and literary artist recast certain, possibly oral traditions, perhaps even his own homilies, in a situation of conflict, crisis, and alienation.[26] The evangelist's purpose in stories like those of Nicodemus (ch. 3) and the blind man (ch. 9) is to show that confessing "faith in Jesus in the full Johannine sense requires a break with rival forms of Jewish belief."[27] A succession of borderline groups in the social environment of the Jn community are addressed: Jews who do not believe in Jesus (2:14–22); the secret Christian Jews (2:23—3:21); the followers of John the Baptist (3:22–26); finally, the Samaritans.[28] None of this hypothesizing is new but it is put forward with brevity and persuasiveness. Rensberger places Nicodemus among the Jewish rulers who were among the crypto-believers in the divinely sent teacher Jesus, but who did not possess the faith adequate to a full and open confession.[29] This Pharisee is seen as a communal symbolic figure because he and Jesus both use the plural of direct address (3:2, 7, 11–12).

Rensberger's special contribution is his insistence on the corporate nature of belief in the FG, neither individualist nor "spiritual." In addition he sees baptism "from above" and eating Jesus' flesh and drinking his blood as symbols of the community's christology, which serve as thresholds or limits of membership. He exegetes the pertinent pericopes carefully (3:5; 3:22—4:1; 6:51c-58) to show that any theory of interpolated passages betraying a sacramental outlook is at odds with the author's conviction about symbol as the vehicle of faith. Removing the disputed eucharistic passage of ch. 6 above, for example, would make problematic why the disciples should have departed after the "hard" words of vv. 60–71. The elimination would further require that the phrase "the flesh is no benefit" be an interpolation responding to an interpolation.[30] The "abiding" in Jesus of 6:56 by eating and drinking him (cf. 14:20 and "even more strongly" 15:4–7) suggests that the "life" that follows results from maintaining the Johannine christological confession.[31] Mutual love is communal solidarity against a hostile world that either does not believe in Jesus or believes otherwise in him.

Rensberger shows how Jn uses the trial scene before Pilate to assert the power of Israel's God, and the one sent by God, over the world's certainties. He finds in it, contrary to the usual assertion of the evangelists' apologetic concern, a fine disregard of confrontation with Rome. All that has preceded in his study leads to a chapter relating certain interests important to Jn to the contemporary problems of the liberation of black people, women, the poor and other oppressed groups. The FG at first appears the least promising of the four for the purpose because it lacks Jesus' radical social and economic pronouncements. Rensburger sees in the gospel, however, the product of a religiously oppressed community that had, at the same time, held on to a form of anti-Roman Jewish messianism.[31] He views baptism in Jn (ch. 3) as a dangerous social relocation for those who make the change and Johannine christology as presenting a Jesus for the oppressed because of the community's perception of itself in that role. Accepting baptism on the terms of Johannine faith in Jesus meant a realignment of the ruler class of teachers with "the accursed," a band of radicals, fanatics "who did not know the law" (7:49)—in brief, a move from the role of persecutors to persecuted.[32]

Such a reading of the FG finds support in the seminal contribution of Wayne Meeks, perhaps the most frequently cited article of the past two decades, which sees in Jn's Jesus an alien, a stranger, "from above," "not of this world."[33] Jn's "sectarianism" is taken by Rensberger to mean a minority counter-culture consciously opposed to much of the status quo in its environment. This makes it a serviceable paradigm for all social situations where a faith commitment underlies resistance to an oppressive majority. The exegete is at pains to point out that nothing of the classical "spiritual" interpretation of the FG is denied, only that besides an individual reading of the experience of believers a social one is demanded by the nature and origin of this gospel.[34]

Depending equally, or more so, on Meeks' interpretation of the Johannine Jesus as a sojourner visiting from heaven, and on anthropologist Mary Douglas' group and grid categories to plot relationships in society, Jerome Neyrey views the FG not so much literarily as sociologically, although one footnote on "point of view" shows his familiarity with some leading studies of narrative.[35] His main concern is to discover the self-image of the community that produced the gospel in its own time and place. Assuming the writing to be a mirror of the struggles of the community and omitting all overt reference to the historicity of events in Jesus' life, Neyrey first devotes four chapters to an exegesis of the Johannine presentation of Jesus as equal to God (5:18; 10:33; 8:24, 28, 58, where "I AM" has no predicate nominative), but not of this world (17:5, 14, 16, 24). Chapters 5, 8, 10 and 11 receive the bulk of attention. The affirmations of Jesus' divinity in 1:1–18, and 20:28 are not explored, Neyrey says, in part because they have been dealt with so frequently, but also because the above four chapters say so much more about Jesus' status and powers as a figure equal to God (Jn's "high christology"). These powers are chiefly two, the power to create (see 5:19–20, with emphasis on "whatever" and "all," and 5:26) and the power to raise the dead and judge them on the last day (5:21–29). Neyrey finds the latter pericope functioning as a "characteristic Johannine topic sentence." It serves as the agenda for developing the "new eschatological predications made of Jesus in John 8, 10, 11."[36] Verses 5:17–29 of themselves provide "convincing proof" that they "reflect a later redaction of 5:10–16, 30–47," focusing on a Johannine high christology.[37] They belong to the same period as the addition of 1:1–18 and 20:28 to the FG, all featuring Jesus' equality with God.[38]

Verses 8:12–20 reflect an earlier tradition, which depicts Jesus as a plaintiff "defending his actions on the Sabbath against hostile Jews"; vv. 21–30, however, portray him as a judge speaking only as the Father has taught him, vv. 49–50 as one who deserves honor

equal to God's, and vv. 51–53 as the giver of post-mortem life.[39]
The three passages are taken to be the result of later redactional
activity, a process that Neyrey will find operative in two stages in
ch. 11.

But first, ch. 10. Verses 1–27 contain Jesus' basic parables, the
popular judgment on him, and the forensic defense of his claims.
These are thought to represent "the replacement stage" of composition, which names him the authentic successor of all the Jewish
ritual and inauthentic shepherding that preceded him. Verses 28–
30, prepared for by 17–18, represent new claims: having life in
himself and being equal to God. Both are the result of later re-
dactive development. The two stages of editing in the ch. 11 Lazarus story—at base, a synoptic-like account of a resuscitation
miracle—were, first, the adjustment required to meet "the death
of Jesus' beloved disciple" (meaning Lazarus), whom some under
the influence of texts like 11:26 had thought deathless ("Whoever
lives and believes in me shall never die"; see also 8:52), and "still
another redaction in which Jesus' eschatological power over death
was demonstrated (11:4, 25)."[40]

These citations should convey adequately Neyrey's technique
in what he calls "traditional methods of exegesis." Anything that
describes Jesus as more than the messiah, a prophet, or an agent of
God's power was added in a second or middle stage. Attribution to
him of the exclusively divine powers of creation and eschatological
judgment were more likely proper to a third stage. Primary were
those presentations of Jesus that propagated the Christian mission,
the middle stage being that which showed him replacing the Jewish
patriarchs, rites, and cultures. The Weston School of Theology
exegete simply cites the researches of those who have theorized on
sources in Jn without calling upon their contributions. His reconstructions are, practically speaking, entirely his own. The principle
is simple. A new redaction is posited for each perceived set of
claims for Jesus' powers and, at the end, an editing in a corrective
spirit.

This prepares the reader for the second of two parts in *An
Ideology of Revolt,* "Not of This World. Christology in Social Science Perspective." In the categories of Mary Douglas, when a
"group" conforms to society's definitions, classifications, and eval-

uations it is said to be "strong," but increasingly weaker as societal pressure on the group decreases. "Low grid" rising to "high" is the description of the socially constrained adherence normally given by a group's members to a prevailing symbol system. Thus, the Johannine church in its early stages would have viewed Jesus as a member of the Jewish covenant community (see Jn 17:3; 1:45; 5:39; 7:40–44, 52), a "strong group" situation, but then it remembered the way he challenged structured life in Israel—a "low-grid" situation regarding sabbath observance and the like.[42] Such is the first stage of the gospel's composition, which Neyrey labels the time of "missionary propaganda." In stage two, called "replacement," Jesus is presented as true temple, cult and feast at the center of a community that is increasingly elitist. Stage three is the period of "high christology" (weak group/low grid) in which spirit is celebrated over matter (6:63), individual personality takes over from group (branches attached to the vine are given as an example of immediate access to Jesus), no ritual behavior is prescribed (again, 6:63), and sin becomes a matter of personal and interior decision (8:24; see 13:8).

The Life-Setting of the Fourth Gospel: From Brown to Neyrey

It was Raymond E. Brown who set the terms for reconstructing the life of the Johannine church in his deceptively simple *The Community of the Beloved Disciple*, originally papers—some of them presidential addresses—before learned societies.[44] He plotted the tension he discerned in the text of the FG, which were chiefly with the community's neighboring Jewish population and other believers in Jesus over the matter of its high christology. A deeper exploration of the subsequent course of community events is found in his Doubleday Anchor commentary on the letters.[45]

Neyrey identifies the introduction of Mary Douglas' anthropological model into Judaic studies with a book of Jacob Neusner on purity in ancient Judaism (1975). Bruce Malina, however, seems to be the pioneer in adapting her work to New Testament studies.[46] Neyrey, having done a few preliminary articles, turns himself over thoroughly to her method of inquiry. He sees the dichotomous patterns in Jn of heaven vs. earth, spirit vs. flesh, from above vs.

from below, and not of this world vs. of this world as boundary-setting categories between the followers of Jesus and the synagogue and even some apostolic-age Christians. (The beloved disciple vs. Peter figures in the same way.[47]) In stages one and two, respectively the period of signs and the period of replacement, the Johannine community's reforming intent brought it into contact with the synagogue on terms of competition and conflict. First the Christians' claims needed defending, then true rites had to replace obsolete or false ones; initially the criteria for leadership were in need of reform, then the reality of ritual. In stage three, the period of high christology, no value is seen in earth or flesh, only heaven and spirit. "The telltale evidence of this is 6:63 and 8:23 in which all value is placed not in material rites or in anything fleshly, earthly, or material, but in spirit alone."[48] Reform is deserted for revolt against all former structures, criteria, and systems. Expulsion from the synagogue (9:22; 12:42) led to the Jn group's physical relocation but also to a new, cosmological placement "above," "not of this world." These recurring changes of location and value were symbolized by the pairing of spirit over matter, flesh, and body. Confessing Jesus as "equal to God" shares the posture of revolt against all systems, whether of the synagogue or the apostolic churches. The triumph of spirit over matter is complete.

Nowhere does Neyrey declare the FG in its final form a gnostic document, nor does he claim Ernst Käsemann's parentage for his theorizing.[49] It is as if Mary Douglas' vocabulary of purity and liminality, strong/weak bodily control replicating strong/weak social control, and sin as corrupting pollutant or as a matter of personal, interior decision seeks perfect expression and finds it in the FG. As with John A.T. Robinson's germ of an idea, a fruitful theory of limited application seems to have taken control of the gospel in its three stages, previously arrived at. Again and again a certain few texts are called on to support a pre-determined structure.

Okure's Contextual Method: Successive Missions of the Son and the Disciples

A study done by a Nigerian exegete does not so much challenge the assumption of Neyrey and others that each redaction of the gospel originated with meeting the special needs of the community addressed, as let the FG dictate its own hermeneutical principles, paying attention to *what* is being said in the final text, *how,* and, speculatively, *why.*[50] Teresa Okure calls her method of study "contextual," contrasting it with stopping at a search for sources and successive editings but not ruling out dialogue with such theories of composition. By contextual she means a combination of rhetorical and literary analysis in the quest for theological meaning, viewed from the standpoint of the evangelist (final author) and what is presumed to be his intended audience.[51] One passage of the canonical text will thus be used to highlight another, part speaking to part. The dialectic going on among passages in the FG is taken to be its intended rhetorical mode (as stressed by Schnackenburg, Brown, Dodd and others), not a matter of contradictions unresolved by the editing process. The contextual method presupposes a reasonably consistent use of terms by Jn and so looks for meaning in disputed passages by recourse to usage in both the immediate context and other parts of the gospel (as with "to labor," "to speak/[her]say-so," and "to testify" in Jn 4, which the book chooses for exegetical treatment, at vv. 6, 38; 26, 42; 30). This "listening approach" to the various levels of Johannine rhetoric is by no means an historicism, although it incorporates historical meaning synchronically with the literary and the theological.[52] The study seeks, overall, to offer a unified interpretation of the evangelist's conception of mission, as indicated by the title.

Much contemporary scholarship in the German and Romance languages has confined the term mission (the word is the same in the two language groups) to bringing the gospel to unbelievers in the erroneously termed third world, while favoring "sending" for its occurrence in Jn. Okure's major thesis is that mission properly describes the sending of the Son by the Father and the Son's sending of the disciples to proclaim him Christ and Son of God to believers and any who may come to believe. She is aware of the propriety of rendering *pempein* and *apostellein* by "send" but finds much of modern scholarship insensitive to the missionary dialectic in Jn between the audience and the one sent which reaches its climax in 20:30–31. That is an explicit statement of the FG's purpose in evangelistic terms. Okure wants the gospel to be seen in that way, since for her these are the only terms on which the evangelist presents it. Few experts in Jn today see it as a missionary tract directed to Jews or Gentiles. Most find it written for a believing community, some holding for Samaritans as a secondary audience. The question is: Do the evident apologetic, polemic and parenetic motifs in Jn disqualify it as having a missionary purpose, a term redolent in today's world of pagan populations?

There is widespread agreement that the Johannine community had a missionary interest in its first stages. Many think, however, that this concern lost out in a community that was in its final stages closed, sectarian, and inward-looking, delivering polemic tirades against its enemies. Okure holds that these views, coupled with those that see a primarily soteriological or eschatological significance in the sending of the Son, tend to obscure the evangelist's understanding of mission.[52] Only this, she thinks, accounts for the gospel's constant choice of Jesus' interaction with his audience in the form of dialogues in which the characters are never mere foils, and discourses. In both he is the one sent and the sender. His mission from the Father is primary and is paralleled by his sending his friends on the identical mission, "that you may believe . . . and that believing you may have life. . . ." The mission of the Paraclete is scarcely dealt with in this study (only on p. 32). The Holy Spirit as a witness to Jesus (along with the Baptist) fares only slightly better.

Three long chapters are devoted to an exegesis of Jn 4:1–42. A survey of authors reveals that, whatever is thought of the origins of vv. 31–38 in the text, most start with the understanding that mission in the passage refers only or primarily to the post-Easter activity of the disciples. Okure counters with the working hypothesis that all of vv. 1–42 deals with Jesus' mission from the Father but from three different perspectives. These are the outlook of the non-believing woman (1–26 [27], the *narratio*), the disciples, whom Jesus instructs in the nature of their involvement in mission (31–38, the *expositio*), and the normative character of Jesus' mission based as it is on the relationship between the missionaries and those they bring to faith in Jesus (28–30; 39–42, the *demonstratio*). The structural relationship of parts may be compared to that of a *semēion* and its explanatory discourse.

Another chapter analyzes vv. 7–26 for the relation of the
themes of salvation as God's gift for the asking and the identity of
Jesus as the Christ appointed by God to dispense it; the rhetorical
devices employed (philosophic persuasion rather than forensic at-
tack, irony); and the passage's missionary features, chiefly Jesus'
manner and method of approach to the woman, his respect for her
as a person rather than as a member of a hostile group, and her
being led to discovery of what "the gift of God" might mean. The
"consequential argument" of vv. 31–42 that follows on the "thesis"
of 1–26 shows Jesus as the one who alone sows with the Father in a
"work" that is the new world order brought about by his mission.
The eschaton is the new time order in which this new world order
operates. In Jn it is a reality that spans both the sowing and the
harvesting phases of the "work." Johannine eschatology is essentially realized eschatology, in Jesus' mission realized both in believers (as life) and in unbelievers (as judgment).

The division of the pericope into its three main parts (vv. 7–
26; 27, 31–38; 28–30, 39–42) reveals three distinct moments in the
missionary enterprise but should not mask the literary and thematic unity of 4:1–42. Essential to the missionary undertaking is
the interaction between the one sent and his audience, which has
as its purpose to evoke a faith response to the divine agent and his
message. Mutual exchange between Jesus and his dialogue partners seems threatened by the *double entendre* in which Jesus understands a reality above nature to be in question when his partner is
operating at the level of nature. But the audience has not been left
behind by this literary technique. A divine being striding the earth
has not been inserted, leaving the revealer and his message as all
that matters (Wrede, Bultmann, Käsemann). Instead, the effort is
made to use language meaningful to the audience to convey realities in the heavenly realm that are within their grasp.[53] Almost all
of the narrative sections and asides in this chapter deal with the
different situations of conflict, missionary and social, which under-
lie it and relate to the situation of the evangelist and his audience.

It is perhaps erroneous to classify Okure's study as literary on
a par with those of Culpepper, Duke and O'Day. Like Thompson's
and those in the chapter to follow, it might better be viewed as the
treatment of a single Johannine theme. Similarly, Neyrey's work is

concerned with one thing, the practical effects in the community of the increasingly heightened christology. Yet all six research pieces have in common a new awareness of the literary product, i.e. the text we have in hand, as it relates to the circumstances in the life of the community that begot it.

4
Treatments of Johannine Themes

Anyone who chooses for scrutiny one aspect or a cluster of related themes in the FG runs the risk of being charged with neglect of equally important themes. But since no one can discuss anything under all aspects at the same time, the writer who isolates a Johannine concern is not to be faulted. Attention to any segment of John's thought brings in its train so much besides, that exploring even a brief pericope poses for the author the problem of where to stop. Most solve the problem by citing a wide range of literature that falls outside their immediate field, both as a way of directing readers further and assuring peers that they are aware of all the opinions they did not incorporate. This final chapter needs to consider the treatments of several individual themes or problems in the FG. Invariably, if the works are of book length they will touch on many other questions.

The Spirit in Jn as God's Power at Work in Jesus/the Risen Christ

Such a work is Gary Burge's dissertation presented to the University of Aberdeen under the supervision of Professor I. Howard Marshall.[1] Its absorption in the questions of the Paraclete (four times in Jn), the Spirit of truth (three times), and more broadly the Spirit (eleven times with the article, seven without; Holy Spirit, without the article twice, with once), at first gives the impression that this will be yet another word study providing unavoidable conclusions in academic form. It proves to be much more encompassing and richer than that. The Paraclete problem is tackled first (see 14:16, 26; 15:26, 16:7; 1 Jn 2:1). The traditional meaning of the word in its few pre- and extra-Christian usages is "intercessor" or "helper," only rarely "legal advocate." Jn employs it, not entirely to describe a replacement figure for the glorified Christ (who continues to be present to the disciples), but as one through whom Christ speaks as he directs the Paraclete's revealing activity. In the era of the church the Paraclete is a forensic or "juridical Spirit . . . giving evidence before the world in [the form of] unique revelations. As Christ was on trial and revealed the Father, so too the disciples (and the Paraclete) were on trial, and in their witness they glorified and revealed Christ."[2] Jesus' glorification alone made the Spirit available (2:39; 19:30, 34).

Burge cites favorably and at length two Catholic scholars in this connection, F. Porsch[3] and I. de la Potterie.[4] Porsch believes that "revelation—the close connection between Spirit and word—is John's overarching message."[5] Jn 6:63 is a pivotal text for him. "From the fact that Jesus gives the Spirit . . . it is established that he speaks God's words. . . . *The giving of the Spirit and the speaking of the word of God* are not two different acts . . . but are . . . as a single event. Since Jesus speaks the words of God or reveals (*lalei*) he also gives the Spirit at the same time."[6] Porsch sees in 3:34, too, Jesus as the giver of the Spirit in speaking God's words.

The primacy of the word is indeed central to Johannine pneumatology, Burge concedes, but he thinks that the emphasis of Jn on *pneuma* as achieving the unique anointing of the messiah is the gospel's greater concern (Jn 1:32, 33, based on Is 42:1). The christological concentration of Jn's pneumatology is assured whether revelation or anointing takes precedence, but Burge finds the indwelling of the Spirit that follows Jesus' anointing paramount. Examining the part the Spirit plays in Jesus' ministry in Jn, Burge discovers it to be God's dynamic, mysterious power working in him, before his exaltation especially, but also after it, "Jesus living powerfully within the community and continuing his work among his followers."[7] In the account of Jesus' baptism (1:29–34), John's experience of the Spirit is described but his baptizing Jesus is not mentioned. The Spirit's empowering of Jesus (vv. 32, 33) is most important for Jn. The dove—a tradition deriving, Burge thinks, from Is 11:2 (where the spirit of the Lord rests on the shoot from Jesse's stump)—confirms Jesus as God's chosen one (v. 34).

Once anointed by the Spirit, the Johannine Christ is not Spirit-impelled to exorcise or perform miracles, as in the synoptics. The power he has comes from God, but the signs he performs reveal not his power but his glory. The miracles are intensely christological in intent. As part of this Spirit christology, "Jesus speaks the words of God ([3]:34a) by virtue of his unlimited anointing in the Spirit. . . . The Spirit is one gift among many (["all things"] 3:35) that Jesus has in full. . . . The Spirit which Jesus immeasurably has will manifest itself in the words he speaks."[9] Jesus has been sent by God to reveal the Father whose gift of the Spirit certifies his revelation. The seal on Jesus of 6:27 is the Spirit, "not a power impulsively resident in Jesus but an attribute of his own person."[10] As Jesus distributes the water alive within him (7:37–38; cf. 4:14), Jn makes clear that this water is Spirit to be dispensed only through the cross (7:39; see 19:34). By the Spirit Jesus is constituted the new temple (2:18–19) from which living waters will flow (see Ez 47:1; Zech 14:8).

"Jesus is the visible presence of the Father, and the life and being of Jesus waiting to be poured forth into the world is the Spirit."[11] This presence is manifested in Jesus' lifetime through his words, which are Spirit and life (6:63). Union with Jesus is depicted in Jn as first appropriating, then remaining in, his word (5:24; 8:51; 14:23; 17:6). Jn's christology of sonship is formed on a prophetic model (see 4:19; 9:17). Jesus is an agent sent by God (sixteen times) but, more than that, he is the Moses-like prophet of the final days (Dt 18:17; cf. Jn 6:14; 7:40). He has manifested God's name (17:6; cf. Ex 3:13–14), his words are equal to scripture (8:28; 17:8), but, most importantly, a centrality is claimed for him that Israel claimed for torah (see 5:39–40, 46–47). Word, prophet and Spirit are brought together in Johannine christology so that it is indistinguishably a pneumatology, in ultimate purpose revelatory of God.

Jn considers 20:22 (Jesus' breathing of the Spirit on his disciples) to be the climax of the relation between them, the fulfillment of their expectation so carefully developed in the farewell discourses. In the two next to last chapters (19—20) Jn brings together the death, resurrection, ascension, and anointing of Jesus in the single event of his glorification, his "hour." The Spirit has been released through the cross. Now Christ and the Spirit must never be separated. The Father bestows the Spirit as an effective encounter with Jesus. The parousia has not been spiritualized, as is so often said. Rather, the Spirit—eternal life (it is one and the same)—now dwells within.[12]

Burge, unlike Bultmann and Protestant scholarship generally, does not think that the pre-redacted Jn has no place for sacraments. Worship of the Father "in Spirit" (4:23) is for him not a rejection of ritualism and ceremony. It is a requirement that all such action refer to a power from God mediated by Christ. This worship is directed toward the flesh and blood of Jesus; the Spirit he supplies will empower it.[13] The community knows Christ in power, Christ in the Spirit. Its anointing with the Spirit means that its members must be on guard against any celebration of baptism or eucharist that does not deepen their experience and knowledge of the Spirit, or instill in the community a sense of unity and love. Worship "in truth" (4:23) *may* mean that which is genuine or grounded in reality but is more likely to be an anticipation of the wisdom christology that sees Christ as the truth (14:6).

Just as Jesus is sent by God, so he sends the Spirit from the Father in a mission identical with that of the disciples acting as the church. The Paraclete sustains the presence of Jesus and effectively enables the church to complete the revealing work of Christ. The Paraclete is advocate and witness to a church enduring persecution, enabling it to speak prophetically. In discussing the Johannine epistles in a brief coda, Burge first maintains that charism is not set entirely in opposition to tradition.[14] He opposes the view of Käsemann and Bornkamm that the epistles represent entrenchment as opposed to expansion, identifying himself with Brown's position that the community required adjustment to a crisis in pneumatology and revelation. Despite this, he accepts their vocabulary of pneumatic vitality vs. catholicism, prophecy vs. tradition. On the basis of the epistolary literature, the missing mean between the extremes would seem to be adhering to the dialectic between anamnesis and inspiration. The tragic opposite of "catholicism" appears to have been departing from the dialectic into communities that opted for the guidance of the Spirit apart from the remembered tradition.

Another View of the Paraclete-Spirit

The question of the Paraclete, which Burge explores in some depth, is dealt with in a full-length study by Bruce Woll in his University of Chicago dissertation *Johannine Christianity in Conflict: Authority, Rank, and Succession in the First Farewell Discourse* (Chico, 1981). The problem he raises is how the Spirit can be depicted so explicitly as a successor figure to Jesus in a gospel that features an otherwise exclusive christology. Is there an authority conflict in the community implicit in the gospel's presentation? And has the Paraclete been erroneously viewed in isolation from the farewell discourses, when their position as one-fifth of the FG, a large quantity of material to be devoted to the *separation* of Jesus from the disciples, requires a harder look? Woll identifies the first farewell discourse as consisting of 13:31–14:31 and discovers there the perception of a threat to the rank and authority of Jesus in the "charismatic competition" of authority figures that came to the fore after his departure. The *preeminence* of the Son and not his *presence* is seen as the theme of this discourse. Woll opts for the separation of Jesus from the disciples and their subordination to him as primary in the introductory section (13:31–14:3), not a word of comfort. Vv. 4–11 are a "capsule summary of the Johannine 'creed' " and correct a fallacy about the departure as requiring the need for replacement.[15] Jesus has not left a vacuum but now exercises his authority on earth from his position in heaven. In vv. 12–24, the disciples are placed in a subordinate position to Jesus, the speaker. Still, they are accorded the high position of successors to him in contrast to the prevailing christocentrism of the gospel. How can they do "greater works" than he (v. 12)? Such promises, Woll thinks, were a "given" of the community's self-understanding, hence too important to be left out; but the author counters the highest boast of these believer-prophets by underscoring their subordination of Jesus. The successor figure of the "Paraclete, the Holy Spirit the Father will send in my name" (14:26) will keep alive Jesus' words, his completed testimony, in his disciples' memory. Hence, no human teaching or authority can replace his, that is to say, the Jesus of the tradition as the author understands it. The Paraclete thus does nothing to disturb the radical christocentrism of the FG but rather confirms it. The disciples mediate Jesus' words and works and are dependent on them. The "Paraclete-Spirit becomes, within the discourse, the form in which Jesus returns to his disciples to mediate their access to the Father."[16] The deduction Woll makes from the discourse is that some in the community were claiming direct access to the Spirit. The gospel's author responds that only Jesus has an unmediated relation to the Father and this the Paraclete confirms. The charismatic authority of Jesus as preeminent is thus affirmed, both in his lifetime and after his departure. The same direct dependence on gifts of the Spirit that he claimed has been claimed by his successors and has gotten out of control. The first farewell discourse has a polemical edge as it supplies a corrective.

Jesus on Trial in Jn over Fidelity to Torah

The year 1975 saw the appearance of a lengthy portion of a dissertation by a Canadian diocesan priest entitled *The Law in the Fourth Gospel.*[17] Severino Pancaro submitted it to the Münster faculty, writing under the direction of Joachim Gnilka. The subtitle in the note below gives some indication of the explicit character of its 571 pages. Viewing Jn as a report on the life and faith of a specific community, probably ethnically Jewish in a much larger Jewish milieu, Pancaro explores carefully the passages that show Jesus charged with being a violator of the sabbath and of the law: with being a sinner (5:1–18; 9; 9:16, 24); a blasphemer (5:17–18; 8:58; 10:24–38); a false teacher who leads people astray (7:14–18, 45–49; 9:24–34; 18:19–24); and an enemy of the Jewish people (11:47–52). This succession of torah-challenges gives the entire gospel a juridical character, making a hearing before Caiaphas the high priest needless (because the outcome was predetermined, 11:49–52; but see 18:24, 28). Jesus cannot be right in the face of these charges, from the point of view of his adversaries at law, "the Jews," and he cannot be wrong from the standpoint of the believing community. The opposition to him does not have the faith required to see in him someone "from God" who must work even as his Father works, who does not blaspheme when he claims to be the Son of God or equal to God, who leads no one astray but only along the same path as Moses. Jesus summons successive witnesses on his behalf: the Baptizer, his works, the revelation made to Israel, the scriptures. None of these will do, for as Jonathan Swift once said of embattled neighbors trading compliments over a back fence, they were arguing from different premises. The disciples of Jesus cannot view anything ever again as do those who call themselves the disciples of Moses. The physical proximity of the two groups that would become synagogue and church only heightens the drama. According to the law, as viewed from a certain perspective, Jesus has to die (19:7; cf. 18:32) and his followers have to be persecuted.

Pancaro asks: For whom would the apologetic tack taken by Jn, i.e. basing Jesus' authenticity on the law in response to a charge of total disregard of it, be meaningful? A Jewish audience is his answer, in a struggle between the Johannine church made up of "Jewish-Christians toward the end of the first century" and " 'normative' Judaism."[18] *Ho nomos* in Jn for him always means torah, the law, in its most comprehensive sense. "Your law" (8:17) or "their law" (15:25) signals dissociation and distancing but not opposition, except insofar as Jesus is above the law through having fulfilled it by his Father's will. In that sense his followers too thought themselves beyond it because of their association with him. The law retains all its value for Jesus and those who believe in him but they have given it the value he assigned it, namely of a witness to him. It is "your" or "their" law only in the sense that it is the law to which Jn's "Jews" appeal. To be of the Johannine community with its christological faith is to know what the scriptures mean and what Moses signified in the history of the Jewish people. For Jn, all have a Christ meaning.

A much briefer book along the same lines appeared in England a year later by A.E. Harvey of King's College, London and St. Augustine's College, Canterbury.[19] He assumes that the author of the FG possessed many of the same data from the tradition as the synoptics but opted to arrange them as a trial of Jesus, conducted by Jewish authority and spread over his public life. Harvey suggests strongly that that was probably what happened in Jesus' history. In a ten-page postscript he states that even if Jn employed the literary form of a lawsuit or *ribh,* the episodes reported are not rendered altogether unhistorical by that fact. This is a considerable backing off from the intimation of the first 122 pages that all happened largely as described.

The FG must have been written for people who understood the legal procedures involved, Harvey thinks. Hence its audience was probably an intermediate culture between Jews and Gentiles that would have known the literary convention of argument as in a court of law, like that found in Job and the prophets. "But again, the Jewishness of this Christian community may well not have been the most significant thing about it."[20] The author concludes he must leave open the question of whom the gospel was written for, in part because of the textual uncertainty of John 20:31, "that you may continue to believe," *pisteuēte* (pres. subj.) or "come to believe," *pisteusēte* (aor.). His final judgment is that it probably was not a missionary book but a book for believers to help them pass judgment, again and again, on the proposition not presented as an established fact that Jesus is the Christ, the Son of God.[21]

Harvey has no interest in the Roman trial that ended in a sentence of death. He assumes that Jesus was condemned by Jewish law on charges of sabbath-breaking and blasphemy and that the Roman prefect crucified him only because the Jews at that time could not, although "In reality it [viz. their citing their incapacity to pass capital sentence by Roman decree; see 18:31] may have been in the nature of an excuse."[22] Jewish legal authority, thwarted in its attempts to put Jesus to death, brought him to Pilate as a person seditious against the Roman state. But this was a totally implausible charge in light of the record about him.[23] St. Paul is cited at Gal 3:13 as part of the evidence that Jesus died on a Jewish charge and therefore accursed in the eyes of the law. Presumably a civil condemnation that resulted in crucifixion would not have achieved this. Harvey cites those whom Jn calls on to testify that Jesus is the Son of God: John (1:19–20, 30–34; 3:28), Nathanael

(1:49), the woman and the townspeople of Samaria (4:19, 42), and Simon Peter (6:69). To these are later added the Paraclete and the disciples (15:26–27). He makes much of the fact that Jewish law did not settle cases on evidence but on the testimony of witnesses, even a single witness of high character. God, too, could be summoned to witness the truth of what was said.[24]

In Harvey's reconstruction qualified "judges" were everywhere in the society, so that if Jesus were drawn into making a self-incriminating statement they could turn a hearing into a "trial."[25] The brief discussion of offenses against the sabbath and blasphemy rely on the Bible and what the Mishnah had made of the pertinent texts by the year 180, as if the two between them tell us how these cases were being judged in the year 30. Jesus' defense is spelled out as given in three places in the gospel: 5:16–18, where "persecute" is taken to mean "prosecute" and he complains (v. 43) that his accusers do not accept him as coming in his Father's name; 10:38, in which he presents the evidence of his deeds; 11:42, where he prays aloud before calling Lazarus forth so that the crowd may believe that God has sent him. The defense is of no avail because, although Jesus' judges follow correct procedures, the verdict has already been passed. Jesus has been testified to as God's agent but is condemned nonetheless. The Paraclete will act thereafter on his friends' behalf, not as an advocate (for Jewish law knew no such role), but to remind and help them speak persuasively (14:16, 26), even as Jesus fulfills the task of advocacy in heaven (1 Jn 2:1). Yet powerful as Jesus may be as counselor, the disciples may not be believed, even as he was not.

Harvey is hampered in the case he makes by modern ignorance of Jewish judicial procedure in the 30s but this does not deter him. Imagination closes in all gaps. One emerges from his tour de force clear on one point at least, that Jn employed the language and techniques of the rabbinic court to build the case against Jesus. The condition of all this, he acknowledges, is that it may well have been the Johannine community and not Jesus who was thus subjected to trial. One must conclude, after wrestling with Pancaro's dense philological and historical argumentation and following Harvey's imaginative reconstruction with a fraction of the same materials, that the former yields the more dependable results.

Johannine Christology, Soteriology, and Meaning of "Son of Man"

Robin Scroggs devotes five short chapters of a book to a summary statement of Jn's christology.[26] Despite certain shortcomings dictated by brevity it is remarkably successful. The Union Theological Seminary professor grants that there is a juridical flavor to much of Jn's theology. He examines the claim and counterclaim regarding Jesus in chs. 6—10 in a section headed "Jesus' Earthly Credentials."[27] Ultimately, he senses that the Johannine community did not do very well in this sustained debate: "At the deepest level . . . there is no adequate earthly proof or demonstration. The outsiders simply cannot grasp the truth while the insiders already know it."[28]

Scroggs says that Jn chose the story form rather than that of the treatise to expose the implicit tension between Jesus and torah—a torah still in some sense honored by Jn's community—because the reality of the Father could only be "experienced" in the person of Jesus, never grasped in proposition form. It had to be "seen," revealed as it was in the ambiguity of flesh. The plot arrangement of Jn's theological narrative seems chronological but is in fact thematic: the enfleshed logos, revealing God in Jesus; "the Son" (thirty-nine times) a complete revelation of the will of "the Father" (one hundred and twenty times) rather than the two in substantive relation; Jesus' self-giving unto death the clearest revelation of God and thus the glorification of both God and Jesus; and the act of the Paraclete enfleshed through the act of the church.

A final chapter exposes eternal life as knowing the divine reality, and asks whether the "indwelling" statements of 14:17 and 23 are so similar to the mutual indwelling of Father and Son (v. 10) that a human participation in the divine is intended. Scroggs recognizes the possible affront to Christian sensibilities in seeing in the "many mansions" pericope, not Jesus going off to heaven to ready a place for faithful disciples, but an eschatological participation in the realm of the Father here and now. This is not an ontological, mystic union of God and the creature but an affective one. Jn seems to attend little to emotional expression but he is totally given to experience of the divine. Does this gospel teach predestination?

Free decision is certainly important (see 3:18–21; 14:23; 15:6) but the divine initiative is equally featured (17:2, 6, 7, 9, 24). Scroggs comes down on the side of the gospel's "fecund ambiguity."[29] His performance is, on several counts, an impressive one.

Two studies of substance that appeared in the mid-1970s are the doctoral dissertations of J. Terence Forestell, a Canadian Basilian,[30] and Francis J. Moloney, a Salesian of Don Bosco from Australia.[31] The theses were defended, respectively, before the Pontifical Biblical Commission and the University of Oxford. Forestell observes that, while the most prominent theology of salvation in the NT sees Christ's death as expiatory for our sins, restoring humanity thereby to the friendship of God (synoptics, Acts, Rom 3:25, but especially Heb), Jn avoids all language of satisfaction or cult. The FG instead presents Jesus' death as integral to the revelatory process in which God is self-manifested, bestowing the divine life on all who believe in Christ (Jn 5:24). Only 1:29 could indicate the expiatory character of Jesus' death, but it is not developed in Johannine fashion and may come from the eucharistic celebrations of the community.[32] The cross is the culminating act in the revealing process, being the exaltation and glorification of the Son of Man. The reception of the word-become-flesh is life-giving but it is not merely the words or works of Jesus that produce this life, it is his very person as the manifestation of the Father. The manifestation is complete when he lays down his life, thereby revealing to believers God's life-giving love (6:51; 10:11; 11:50, 51; 15:13; 18:14). The preposition *hyper* ("for," "for the sake of") occurs throughout but it describes the purpose of his dying, not its cause, and never has sin as its object. This understanding of faith in the cross as saving is not a reduction to gnosis, a mere doctrine about God, both because it is incarnational and because the death is an integral part of the total revelation. This should cause us to rethink the meaning of worship and sacrifice. In Jn, Jesus' sacrifice has become a manifestation of God's word of love and a sanctification of Christ himself.

The Moloney study, done under the direction of Dr. F. Morna Hooker, establishes that "Son of Man" in Jn is always used of the human Jesus—from beginning to end of his career—and always in the third person. A Father–Son of Man relation never occurs. The

Son of Man is the unique revealer of God because only he has ever come down from heaven (3:13; 6:62). As Son of Man he is a judge; he is lifted up in crucifixion; he is glorified on the cross. His hour has arrived as he goes to the cross (12:23, 34; 13:13; 19:5). When the word became flesh it became Son of Man, not a convenient messianic term in Jn but an explanation of why Jesus is in the world: to reveal God. Jn has taken the term from the Christian tradition, which in turn derived it from Dan 7:13. There, one like a son of man comes before the Ancient of Days in company with the saints, to be given dominion and everlasting kingship. Jn presents Jesus under this title as the one by whom the world judges itself, depending on its acceptance or rejection of him.

"Son of Man" originated as a bit of idiomatic self-reference by Jesus, for Lindars. It was not a title and has nothing of the apocalyptic Dan 7:13 about it. Jn derived it from the tradition of a passion saying (see 3:14) and used it to convey "the agent of the revelation which is disclosed in the cross."[33]

The book-length FG scholarship to be reported on ends here, with two exceptions. One treatment of the literary structure of Jn, necessarily hypothetical, will have to stand for the literally dozens of journal articles on the structure of individual pericopes that have appeared in the twenty years under review. It is the work of a Swedish scholar, Birger Olsson.[34] Like many others, he is led by his careful text analysis to see in the gospel a book written for believers, not a missionary tract. The basic message of the two passages he chooses for scrutiny is the way the people of the latter covenant comes to birth from the former, with Samaritans included. Both the Cana story (2:1–11) and that of the Samaritan woman (4:1–42) are told on two levels, narrative and symbolic, with many allusions to biblical and deuterocanonical texts. Chapter 4 is multiply "screened," meaning composed of overlying strata. A basic "*ergon*" screen (the historical deed of Jesus) has had a "well" screen placed over it which draws on the narratives in Gen 29 and Ex 2:15ff. (Rachel and the seven daughters of the priest of Midian at their respective wells).

Ch. 4 was edited finally in such a way as to convey a sense of the gathering in of all the people of God. At the end of Olsson's laborious sleuthing into sources, seams, and first, second and third levels of narration, he asks why the many who concur with him in seeing a narrative level overlaid by successive "screens" require a late date for the final composition. Why could it not all have developed rapidly, giving a much earlier date for Jn than is usually proposed? But this challenge is not the book's chief merit, which rather is to show how a text in the gospel as it stands can be analyzed to reveal how it was constructed, and the internal language clues that suggest its levels of composition.

The second volume in summary is Raymond E. Brown's 840-page commentary on the three letters of John—the first of them like Hebrews actually a treatise.[35] Their importance is that they identify a group of secessionists from the community who show the perils of taking the christology and eschatology of the "GJohn" (his usage throughout) to extremes. Brown says there is no reason not to attibute authorship of all three epistles to the same person, although there is no way to prove that such was the case, and that they seem to come from a period after the evangelist completed his gospel (ca. 90 for Brown) but before the final redactor's work (shortly after 100). Divisions in the community appear to have developed with the crystallizing of Johannine thought in the gospel. This would account for the absence of polemic against *hoi Ioudaioi* of 1 John. There is total absorption with the enemy within, namely those "antichrists" and "liars" (1 Jn 2:18, 22) who do not hold that Jesus is the Christ who has come in the flesh (2 Jn 7). There is nothing in GJohn to require that second century Christians go the way of what became orthodoxy *or* a variety of gnostic heresies (apparently the path of the greater number). Neither can it be supposed that the epistles had only GJohn to go on; there surely was a more ample Johannine tradition (see Jn 21:25).

To follow Brown in his exhaustive treatment of a literature that covers only six pages in an ordinary Bible is to learn much more about the gospel than a study confined to the epistles would yield. He generously suggests on an early page that the material in his Introduction—which he proposes should be read both before and after the bulk of the book—and his Notes after each pericope, should provide sufficient aid to scholarly readers in arriving at other positions than those adopted in the extended Comment that follows the Notes.

A Selection of Articles from the Periodical Literature

Much of the better Johannine scholarship in English-language journals of the last twenty years has subsequently been incorporated into the books noted above. The selection made here will be guided chiefly by positions taken that were not previously reported on in these pages. Certain research pieces have been omitted because of their technical nature, although some of those summarized below are philologically sophisticated but relatively easy to follow in their argument. The first articles summarized are concerned with problems touching the gospel generally and are listed alphabetically by author. The remainder are in the sequence in which the matters they discuss occur in Jn.

1. Jouette M. Bassler, "The Galileans: A Neglected Factor in Johannine Community Research," *CBQ* 43, 2 (April 1981), 243–57. The Southern Methodist University scholar sees Jn employing "Galileans" (in fact, Jesus' initial followers) to symbolize those who receive the word, "Judeans" those who reject it. The hearers whose response is favorable are always designated, sometimes intrusively and awkwardly, as "Galileans." With time, the escalating claims for Jesus bring some who were initially receptive to a neutral or negative stance. Thus, in ch. 6 some disciples move from the ranks of "Galileans" back to "Judeans" (6:60–66). If the "*Ioudaioi*" of chs. 5 and 9 represent opposition, the "*Galilaioi*" of 4:43–54 represent acceptance.

2. F.-M. Braun, "La Réduction du Pluriel au Singulier dans l'Evangile et la Première Lettre de Jean," *New Testament Studies* 24, 1 (Oct. 1977), 40–67. Only someone steeped in the texts of the Johannine writings like this Belgian Dominican exegete of "John the Theologian" is likely to have tracked down the tendency (seven times in the gospel, three times in 1 Jn) represented by: utterances/ word, works/work, commandments/commandment, sins/sin, those things/all [that I gave], antichrists/antichrist, disciples/disciple. Braun concludes that an author, not a redactor, is responsible for this powerful conception of simplicity, "haunted by the need to lead all to unity."

3. John T. Carroll, "Present and Future in Fourth Gospel 'Eschatology,' " *Biblical Theology Bulletin* 19, 2 (April 1989), 63–

69. This brief article not only sketches out the general lines of the much-argued subject of the title but points to the 1967 Ph.D. dissertation of John Thompson and a half-dozen monographs on the subject. Carroll concludes that while 1 Jn gives eschatology a more explicit and significant role than the gospel, the two are similar in the way they present present and future "life." Belief in Jesus and his word is the means to it in the FG, to be persevered in until the "last day."

4. N.H. Cassem, "A Grammatical and Contextual Inventory of the Use of *kósmos* in the Johannine Corpus with Some Implications for a Johannine Cosmic Theology," *NTS* 19, 1 (Oct. 1972), 81–91. *Kosmos* ("world") appears one hundred and five times in all, seventy-eight times in the FG (almost six times more often than in the synoptics), twenty-four in 1, 2 and 3 Jn, three in Revelation. Cassem first analyzes the unmodified uses of the noun, then its appearances with "to," "from," "in," and "concerning." All twelve of the occurrences of the phrase "this world" (eleven in the gospel) denote an incompatibility with Jesus' way of life. The chief finding is that the term is used in a favorable sense in chs. 10—13 but a more ambivalent or hostile one in 14—18, while dropping out in 19—21. All references to "the light of the world" are in the first twelve chapters, as are seventy-percent of the word's directly soteriological contexts. This means that God's view of the world is presented in the first part of the gospel (where "into the world" makes eight of its twelve Johannine appearances), while the world's response to God is given in the second part (twelve of the fifteen total occurrences of "out of the world," all pejorative). Cassem thinks that his statistical proof of the evangelist's intent might serve as the first building block of a Johannine cosmic theology.

5. Douglas K. Clark, "Signs in Wisdom and John," *CBQ* 45, 2 (April 1983), 201–09. The Wisdom in question is the deuterocanonical Wis Sol—if David Winston is right (Doubleday Anchor Bible 43, 1979), a work produced during Caligula's reign (AD 37–41) and a "best seller" among diaspora Jews. Its chs. 11—19 are a midrashic rereading of Moses' dealings with the pharaoh in Exodus. Wis does not give ten plagues but six *sēmeia* (10:16), each consisting of a plague and a balancing benefit to the Israelites (see 11:15).[36] The drowning of the pharaoh and his army is a seventh

extraordinary event that surpasses all the others. Clark reckons six signs in Jn, not counting the walking on water as distinct from the loaves, and as the seventh extraordinary sign Jesus' lifting up in death and resurrection. Clark finds correspondence in all the signs but the second, the royal official's son and the frogs (Wis 11:15; 16:1–4). He may or may not be on to something Jn had in mind but he is at least alert to deuterocanonical influence on the NT, a matter until lately widely disregarded.

6. Edwin D. Freed, "Egō Eimi in John 1:20 and 4:25," *CBQ* 41, 2 (April 1979), 288–91. Not so much a claim that the Johannine "I am" in these two places (and 3:28), used absolutely, is a title of the Christ—this is assumed—but that its appearance in Mk 13:6 and 14:62, likewise Acts 13:25 (the Baptist's denial that he is the "I am" the crowds suppose him to be), indicates that this was already traditional terminology when Jn employed it, coming from Mk if not earlier.

7. John J. Gunther, "The Alexandrian Gospel and the Letters of John," *Catholic Biblical Quarterly* 41, 4 (Oct. 1979), 581–603. All but three pages are devoted to the gospel, disclosing its abundant parallels to Philo, the Hermetic corpus, and Jewish and Christian apocrypha from Egypt. The large Jewish population there was politically alienated from its neighbors in the years 38–117 C.E. A controversial anti-Jewish tone marks the *Preaching of Peter* (*Kērygma Petrou*) and other early Egyptian Christian writings. Absent from John is any mention of the Sadducees; the "scribes" occurs once. Among Gunther's strongest arguments for an Alexandrian provenance are the early dates of papyri in Egypt containing Jn and their textual cognate, Codex Vaticanus (B), and the third century popularity of the gospel in Egypt (first in order in the original form of the Sahidic NT). The parallels between certain phrases in Jn and assembled Alexandrian *monumenta,* practices, and culture are impressive.

8. George MacRae, "The Fourth Gospel and *Religionsgeschichte*," *CBQ* 32, 1 (Jan. 1970), 13–24. This much-cited short essay steers a middle course in the debate over Hebraic and Hellenic influences on Jn. The late and deeply lamented Jesuit of Harvard University asks whether the various christological titles employed (first catalogued in Jn 1:35–51) and forms of religious

understanding might not have been an attempt to assimilate a variety of religious backgrounds, declaring ultimately that Jesus transcends them all. The gospel's final redactor writes as he does to promote the universality of Jesus, not shrinking from a Helleniza-tion of his Palestinian materials to show the sufficiency of a univer-sal idea in all settings.

9. B.A. Mastin, "A Neglected Feature in the Christology of the Fourth Gospel," *NTS* 22, 1 (Oct. 1975), 32–51. This English scholar holds, against Vincent Taylor among others, that *théos* in Jn does not describe Jesus' function but who he is. "God" is con-sciously employed as one of his titles: in 1:1 it is made equivalent to the pre-existent *logos,* in 1:18 to the incarnate *logos,* and in 20:28 it is not an exclamation by Thomas at a work of God, the resurrec-tion, but an intended attribution of godhead to Jesus.

10. Frans Neirynck, "John and the Synoptics" in M. de Jonge, ed. *L'Évangile de Jean. Sources, rédaction, théologie* (Gembloux/ Leuven, 1977), 73–106. Challenging what amounts to a consensus on Jn's independence of the synoptics since the work of Gardner-Smith (1938), Neirynck first exposes the views of Lindars (1972), Boismard (1972) and Dauer (1972) to the effect that canonical Jn drew, respectively, on sources used by Mk and Lk; on canonical Mt and a previous version of Jn to which an intermediate Mt and a proto-Luke contributed, and Q to both; and on a Johannine prede-cessor of Jn's passion narrative, possibly written, in which some elements of the canonical synoptics were fused with the oral tradi-tion. Since dependence on intermediate sources cannot be proved, Neirynck asks all three authors: Why not dependence on the synop-tics themselves? He chooses Jn 20:1–18 to make the case for direct dependence on Mt 28:9–10 and Lk 24:12, both the editorial compo-sitions of those evangelists with no tradition behind them other than Mk. Neirynck sees the christophany of Jn 20:17 as directly dependent on Mt 28:9–10, the Matthean alternative to Mk's vision of an angel (16:7). Similarly, Lk 24:12 was entirely the evangelist's own composition and Jn followed him in his expanded 20:3–10. Jn's treatment of his sources, Neirynck concludes, consisted in a combination and harmonization of the synoptic accounts.

11. T.E. Pollard, "The Father-Son and God-Believer Rela-tionship according to St. John: A Brief Study of John's Use of

Prepositions," in *L'Évangile de Jean. Sources, rédaction, theolo-gie,* ed. M. de Jonge (Gembloux/Leuven, 1977), 363–70. Assum-ing (but not discussing) that no "ontological" relation can be established between Father and Son in Jn, Pollard says that the gospel is nonetheless clear that the two are in more than a merely moral unity. Jesus is always called "the Son," believers "children" of God. A detailed analysis of the use of "to," "with" and "from" in the various cases they govern provides the finding that the Father-Son relation is extended to believers, of which it is the prototype (14:20). Oepke had called it the " 'in' of fellowship" but it is closer to participation—not, however, absorption in a mystical sense. The participation of believers with Jesus, the only Son, is a matter of a company of believers, not individuals.

12. Sandra Schneiders, "History and Symbolism in the Fourth Gospel," in M. de Jonge, ed. *L'Évangile de Jean. Sources, rédac-tion, théologie* (Gembloux/Leuven, 1977), 371–76. The symbolic and the historical do not occur in inverse proportion, as an article that preceded this Louvain conference paper and another that followed it affirm.[37] Schneiders, a religious of the Immaculate Heart of Mary on a Jesuit theological faculty, maintains that if a text is essentially symbolic it has no literal meaning apart from a symbolic meaning. She defines symbol as the sensible expression of a present reality while sign expresses an absent reality. Much of Jn has an essentially symbolic meaning since Jesus is, for the evan-gelist, the symbolization of God as both revelatory and mediatory. The FG is itself a symbolic revelation, not just a record of a sym-bolic revelation. "It is a literary icon of Jesus." History is used by Jn as symbolic material; the more historical it is seen to be, the more symbolic it will be seen to be. Symbolism is not an element in Jn but its dimension as a whole, i.e. its characteristic revelatory mode. Valid symbolic interpretation is not to be confused with allegorizing. The genuine symbol is polyvalent by nature, not arbi-trary or undemonstrable. There are, hence, numerous valid inter-pretations of symbol but not all interpretations are valid. Criteria exist to interpret symbolic works validly.

13. Elisabeth Schüssler Fiorenza, "The Quest for the Jo-hannine School: The Apocalypse and the Fourth Gospel," *NTS* 23, 3 (July 1977), 402–27. This is a confirmation of the distinct author-

ship of the FG and the vision of John of Patmos for any who may still need it. The Rumania-born Harvard professor brings her expert status on the last book of the NT to bear on what she considers the writings of two non-rival schools of Christianity in the province of Asia. Revelation is rooted in an early prophetic-apocalyptic school; its author has access to Johannine and Pauline traditions (but more of the latter). Near to him are two schools considered dangerous, that of the man called Balaam (2:14) and the woman Jezebel (2:20). The book of Revelation is in no direct literary relation with the FG but one of dialectical exchange. The two take opposite options on the eschatological question but not confrontationally. The outcome is that the eschatology of the prophetic-apocalyptic school modifies that of the gospel.

14. Fernando Segovia, "The Love and Hatred of Jesus and Johannine Sectarianism," *CBQ* 43, 1 (Jan. 1981), 258–72. "Love" and "hate" in this community ultimately mean belief and unbelief in Jesus as messiah and Son of God. Struggle over these matters led the separated group to see itself as basically alientated from "the world," rejecting its values. Who make up this *kosmos?* In 7:1–9 the Judeans who seek to kill Jesus, who cannot follow him (13:33), and refuse to believe in him (14:24). Jn means to separate the elect "children" or "friends" from the parent synagogue, requiring his gospel to be viewed as sectarian and his community as a sectarian group.

Attention to Specific Pericopes in Jn

a. The first of the journal articles to deal with a specific passage in the FG rather than an aspect or theme is P. Joseph Cahill's "The Johannine *Logos* as Center," *CBQ* 38, 1 (Jan. 1976), 54–72. While the term *Logos* for "word" occurs in only two verses of Jn (1:1 [three times]; 14) it pervades the whole and in C.K. Barrett's words comes closest to a thematic utterance. The mythical elements of Jn have been by-passed by historical criticism, Cahill thinks, but they may be the more important ones. The center is "pre-eminently the zone of the sacred, the zone of absolute reality" (M. Eliade, *Cosmos and History*). For the U.S. scholar at the University of Alberta, biblical hierophanies and theophanies occur at the center (ex.: Bethel, Ex 35; Mount Gerizim as navel, Jgs 9:37). The *logos,* the center of primordial unity, existed in primal, archetypal time and "was God." Becoming flesh made of it an exteriorized reality. Humanity thus became the Word's symbol, expressing what is basically inexpressible. Eternal *logos* gives intelligibility to the structure of the FG, Cahill thinks, not "signs" (the first half) or "glory" or "hour" (the second half). The Word permeated the world as light and life. All else—miracles, foreknowledge, judgment on the world, death, and resurrection—are to be understood in the light of *logos* as center. This center is absolute, the source of meaning from which all other meaning is derived. All history will be judged by its posture in relation to the *logos*-center.

b. Thomas B. Dozeman, "*Sperma Abraam* in John 8 and Related Literature," *CBQ* 42, 3 (July 1980), 342–58. Verses 8:30–31 are for this author an editorial insertion into vv. 31–59, a controversy over freedom. Dozeman thinks that "seed of Abraham" in the pericope (vv. 33, 37; "children of Abraham," v. 39) is a technical term describing Christian Jews who advocate a law-observing mission as opposed to law-free believers in the Jn community. Abraham was important apologetically in pre-Christian Judaism, also in Philo and Josephus. Paul uses "seed of Abraham" to describe Christian Jews advocating a law-observing mission in Rom 9:7; 11:1; 2 Cor 11:22. In Justin's *Dialogue* (23–24, 44, 47.4) it has the same connotation, describing some Christians who are persuaded to the legal way of life. In the controversy of Jn 8, "As far as the party of freedom is concerned, to stress the law is to kill Jesus and be outside the community of faith." At issue is truth versus a legal way of life (the opposing parties of the two fathers, God and Abraham in 8:38). Says Dozeman, "The *sperma Abraam* are liars; Jesus speaks the truth."

c. Joseph A. Grassi, "The Role of Jesus' Mother in John's Gospel: A Reappraisal," *CBQ* 48, 1 (Jan. 1986), 67–80. Basic to Grassi's position on the mother of Jesus (Jn never calls her Mary) is acceptance of M. Girard's theory that the seven signs of the FG are structured chiastically (*Studies in Religion / Sciences Religieuses* 9, 3 [1980], 315–24). They include the miracle of the loaves (6:1–71) as the fourth sign at the crossing of the *chi* (χ) but not the walking on water as distinct from it. The "great hour of Jesus: his mother, the cross, and the issue of blood and water from Jesus' side (19:25–37)" constitute the seventh sign. This places the Cana miracle (2:1–12) at the top arms of the χ matching the "great hour" at the bottom. The promised bread/flesh of the Son of Man (6:27, 53, 62) at the center looks back to Jesus' human origins (6:42) and ahead to his giving his mother to the beloved disciple/community (19:26–27) as its mother. "The first and seventh signs carry the common elements of the presence of Jesus' mother, the centrality of the 'hour,' and the focus on obedience[,] as well as the interconnection of water/wine/spirit." Culpepper, untypically among modern Protestant commentators (*Anatomy,* pp. 133–34), and Hoskyns, an Anglican (*Fourth Gospel,* p. 530), likewise seem to see Jesus' mother in this light.

   d. Sandra Schneiders, "The Foot Washing (John 13:1–20): An Experiment in Hermeneutics," *CBQ* 43, 1 (Jan. 1981), 76–92. Departing from the assumption of traditional criticism that its task is to reconstruct the author's meaning for the original audience, and taking the position of contemporary hermeneutics (Gadamer, Ricoeur) that the interpreter of a text must dialogue with it to understand its truth claims, the author sees as one meaning of the foot washing Jesus' work of transforming the sinful structures of domination in society into the model of friendship (neither superiority nor inferiority but equality). Jesus does not provide a model of humiliation or menial service since the entire passion account in Jn reveals his glory. His friendship for his disciples expresses itself in his joyful mutual service unto death. Critical exegesis can be used to analyze the story's various parts (vv. 1–3; 4–11; 12–20) but a hermeneutic proper to our time, with its sensitivity to dominance and subordination in all human relations, discloses this pericope as basically an example of friendship that finds, or makes, two to be equal.

   e. Fernando Segovia, "The Theology and Provenance of John 15:1–17," *JBL* 101, 1 (March 1982), 115–28. The two sub-sections of this segment of farewell discourse, vv. 1–8 and 9–17, are found to present different aspects of inner-community controversy. Jesus as "true vine" discloses a christological debate; the second sub-section points to the dangers of community members' ceasing to abide as "friends" in the hierarchy of love. Segovia is a Vanderbilt

University faculty member who concludes that this chapter was written by the author of 1 Jn or someone in the same situation, then appended after 14:31. Both writings (and 13:34–35 as well) are anti-docetic and distinguish between true and false believers. Verses 1–8 abide in the original proclamation concerning Christ; vv. 9–17 abide in the love command.

f. John W. Pryor, "John 4:44 and the *Patrís* of Jesus," *CBQ* 49, 2 (April 1987), 254–63. For Mk (6:1–6) Jesus' *patrís* is Nazareth, for Lk (4:16–30) Israel as a whole. Each had a different source. What they had in common was the saying of Jesus about a prophet's honor. Jn at 4:44 (a dislocation, since the transition from v. 43 to v. 45 is smooth) resembles Lk (Israel as a whole). Disbelief or misunderstanding of Jesus in Jn is not confined to one location. He has had a successful ministry in Samaria (4:23) and proceeds to Galilee "*qua* part of the total *patrís* Israel." Pryor gives two reasons: in 4:9, 20, 22 Israel *in toto* is contrasted with Samaria, the Judea-Samaria dichotomy of 4:3 yielding to a Samaria-Galilee dichotomy, with the latter standing for the whole of Israel; and Jn 12:36–43 applies to the rejection of Jesus by all Israel. Restricting 4:44 to Galilee would run counter to the overall mind of Jn.

g. Finally, two articles that appeared in the last two decades (although not in the time sequence of the six above) deal with the perennial problem of Jn 21 in relation to the whole gospel, taking the minority position that it came from the evangelist's hand, not a redactor's. Paul S. Minear in "The Original Functions of John 21," *JBL* 102, 1 (March 1983), 85–98 recalls that no MS. has been found without this chapter, the vocabulary, grammatical habits and style of which reflect a high homogeneity with chs. 1–20. Scholars' views of the editorial design and theological outlook of the first twenty chapters *alone* account for the consensus position of a redactor's composition. But, Minear writes, 20:29–31 conclude that chapter more fittingly than they do the whole gospel. Only in ch. 21 is there provided an end to the careers of Peter and the beloved disciple, of whom there is silence in 20:11–31. Chapter 21 has many links to the earlier chapters, notably telling the fate of the flock after Jesus' death and answering the question of 14:22 (and see v. 21) with its account of Peter's profession of love.

h. Stephen Smalley, "The Sign in John XXI," *NTS* 20, 3 (April

1975), 275–88 takes the fact that the subject matter is new to account sufficiently for the twenty-eight words not found in Jn 1— 20. The "After these things" with which ch. 21 begins is not enough reason "for regarding this chapter as non-Johannine. . . . I suspect [it is] . . . from the same hand." Smalley holds that the miraculous catch of fish, which is secondary in Lk 5:1–10 (as v. 11 indicates), is primary in Jn 21:1–14. "The narrative of this sign [in ch. 21] . . . clearly suggests . . . the initial context of a post-resurrection tradition," a sign possessing "the background of a primitive and historically reliable tradition."

Some Helpful Books for Students, Teachers, Preachers

To discover in a fifty-eight-page pamphlet of four chapters a summary of the purpose, literary patterns, and problems of John up to the date of the inquiry is a matter of pleasant surprise, but George MacRae, S.J. has done it in *Faith in the Word. The Fourth Gospel* (Chicago: Franciscan Herald, 1973). He followed it up with the more leisurely *Invitation to John. A Commentary on the Gospel Text from the Jerusalem Bible* (Garden City: Doubleday Image, 1978), 236 pages. After the prologue (1:1–18), MacRae divides the Book of Signs (1:19—12:50) into twenty-nine pericopes for comment and the Book of Glory (13:1—20:31) into twelve, calling 21:1–25 an appendix. The observations are brief and thoroughly dependable.

Two popular presentations of Johannine research have been done by Professor Pheme Perkins of Boston College. The first of these was her *Gospel of St. John* in the Read and Pray series (Chicago: Franciscan Herald, 1975), page-long comments on eighty-eight passages for daily reflection over a three-month period. Her *The Gospel according to St. John. A Theological Commentary* (*idem*, 1978), 251 pages, followed it. Perkins devotes one chapter to each of the twenty-one chapters of the gospel and provides comments on successive pericopes rather than individual verses. Part I is entitled "Calling Disciples" (chs. 1—4); II, "Public Ministry" (5— 12); III, "Farewell Discourses" (13—17); and IV, "Crucifixion/ Resurrection: The Glorification of Jesus" (18—21). Perkins is a woman of deep learning but her exposition makes easy reading.

Stephen S. Smalley, a Church of England scholar, produced in that same year *John: Evangelist and Interpreter* (Greenwood, 1978), 285 pages. He first gives a brief history of Johannine scholarship, then attempts to answer the questions concerning the gospel: who, what, when, where, and why? Smalley opts for a third and final stage of composition at Ephesus by the apostle John, who is the beloved disciple. The treatment is mostly according to themes but there is some step-by-step exegesis, notably of the Cana miracle, the multiplication of the loaves, and the raising of Lazarus. The positions taken might be called historically conservative.

John Painter's *Reading John's Gospel Today* (Atlanta, 1980), 158 pages, is a slighter effort. It appeared formerly as *John, Witness and Theologian* (London, 1975), 160 pages. After an Introduction he devotes Part II to the gospel's theology and Part III to interpreting 1 Jn, with a concluding Part IV on "John's Symbolism. Word Symbol or Sacrament?" in which he holds that symbolism is so broad in Jn that the rites of baptism and eucharist have no exclusive function there. "The evangelist is no sacramentalist in this [viz. Bultmann's] sense" (p. 139). That he might be a sacramentalist in a late first century sense is not taken into account.

Robert Kysar has produced three extremely helpful studies over a decade. The first is *John, the Maverick Gospel* (Atlanta, 1976), 119 pages, reckoned by Scroggs to be the best non-technical introduction to the FG. It is based on the landmark commentaries available at the time in English and is distinguished by its excellence as a pedagogical tool. Another work, simpler but equally enlightening, is *John's Story of Jesus* (Philadelphia, 1984), 96 pages. A diagram on the spiraling character of the Nicodemus discourse is illustrative of the construction of all the discourses. A schematic overview of the signs and speeches of chapters 2 through 5 is another helpful device. The observation that "Jesus' life and ministry are the re-creation of the Jewish faith" (p. 24) is closer to the mark than an earlier observation, "Torah is indeed the revelation of God, but Jesus is the further revelation which supersedes the Law" (p. 18). Two themes are isolated as paramount in Jn's concern: Jesus' transforming and fulfilling of Hebraic tradition, and the role of the witnesses to Christ's truth. Kysar's division of the gospel is interesting: Beginnings (1:1–51);

Jesus Reveals Glory (2:1—12:50); Jesus Receives Glory (13:1—20:29); and Endings (20:30—21:25). Perhaps the most ambitious, although not the most ingenious, of his three books is *John, An Augsburg Commentary on the New Testament* (Minneapolis, 1986), 331 pages. This book "for lay people, students and pastors" is written in running prose and says something about every verse. It has no foreign words or phrases and no footnotes but is remarkably comprehensive.

The Liturgical Press, in replacing its New Testament Reading Guide series of the early 1960s with the Collegeville Bible Commentary, had Neal M. Flanagan, O.S.M., since deceased, do its *The Gospel According to John and the Johannine Epistles* (1983), 128 pages. At the same time, this publisher engaged Raymond F. Brown to reedit *The Gospel and Epistles of John. A Concise Commentary* (Collegeville, 1988), 136 pages, from its earlier NTRG version. Like all the commentaries in both series, those of Flanagan and Brown provide the text of the biblical books on the top of each page. Brown's pamphlet of 1960 had previously been revised in 1965 and 1982. In the 1988 edition the gospel receives an introduction of eleven pages and the epistles, four. The latter, in accord with Brown's Doubleday Anchor Bible 30, *The Epistles of John*, holds that while a disciple of the beloved disciple probably wrote the gospel on the authority of the apostle John, the author of all three letters could have been a presbyter in the Johannine circle. The gospel was edited by a final redactor, mostly by a process of addition. An important liturgical aid for Catholics is the listing of readings from Jn and 1, 2 and 3 Jn in the Roman Lectionary for Sundays, feasts and weekdays. They are given in their sequence in the gospel rather than in the church's calendar. Here, in compendious form, are the major positions to be found in Brown's magisterial three volumes.

He had produced an "updating summary" of his researches on Jn a decade after the appearance of the second volume on the gospel and in anticipation of the book on the epistles then in preparation. This exploration of the development of the Johannine church was entitled *The Community of the Beloved Disciple* (New York/Mahwah, 1979), 204 pages. It stemmed from Brown's presidential address to the Society of Biblical Literature and his Shaffer

Lectures at the Yale Divinity School. He traces hypothetically the progress of a group of Jewish believers in Jesus from a relatively "low" christology (messiah, prophet, servant, Lord, Son of God in the sense of divine representative) to a "high" one (Jesus within the sphere of divinity, Lord and Son of God in a more exalted sense, and even the designation "God"). The leader in this transition was a disciple who would come to be known as "the disciple whom Jesus loved." It was catalyzed by the adherence to the movement of Jews of anti-temple bias who made converts in Samaria and brought on debates with other Jews who thought the movement constituted an abandonment of strict monotheism. Gentile Greeks of the diaspora joined the community. These developments, coupled with the commitment to a high christology against Jews and Jewish Christians of a more traditional faith persuasion, led to a third phase, a split within the community. The adherents of the author of the epistles (the "presbyter") witnessed the departure of the secessionists, calling them children of the devil and antichrists. Their offense was affirming that *knowledge* of God's Son was all-important and denying the full humanity of one who was divine, as he was. Those in the presbyter's party who confessed that Jesus had come in the flesh held that anointing with the Spirit obviated the need for human teachers. They went on to accept presbyter-bishops as authoritative teachers in the second century. This group was gradually assimilated into the great church, while the larger number of the Johannine community seem to have moved to gnosticism of a docetic variety.

D. Moody Smith's *John,* in Fortress' Proclamation series (second rev. ed.; Philadelphia, 1986), 133 pages, is not a verse commentary so much as a treatment of themes, but with exegesis of the prologue (1:1–18), chs. 5, 9, 16, and 1 Jn. An introductory Part I discusses the FG's characteristics and structure, distinguishing between Jesus' public ministry and his ministry to his disciples. After the exegetical portion illustrative of the Johannine perspective past and present comes the final Part III, Interpretation. There, a number of aspects are discussed: historical origins of the gospel, theological factors influencing the development of Jn's thought, and the task of interpreting an interpretation, which the FG is. The revised edition adds to the earliest part discussions of the relation of Jn to the synoptics and also to the epistles, and to the third part an extensive literary analysis.

A number of important Johannine scholars have not appeared in these pages, chiefly because their contributions were made before the twenty-year period of our special interest. Michael J. Taylor, S.J. has compiled an anthology for student use called *A Companion to John. Readings in Johannine Theology* (*John's Gospels and Epistles* (Staten Island: Alba, 1977), 281 pages, in which solid contributions by Marsh, Grossouw, Barrosse, and Feuillet are to be found.

José Porfirio Miranda presents a quirky but not unserious view of Johannine eschatology and the gospel and epistles in *Being and the Messiah. The Message of St. John* (Maryknoll: Orbis, 1977; Spanish original, 1973), 245 pages. The Mexican polymath betrays wide reading habits in this basically anti-Marxist polemic, showing the Johannine final age to be a matter of the "now" of history and not the never-never land the detractors of the New Testament make it out to be. He does not, parenthetically, find *pros* meaning "with" anywhere in Greek literature; this necessitates for him in Jn 1:1 a "word [spoken] *to* God."

Bruce E. Schein, in a quite different direction, takes the reader on a walking tour of the places named in Jn's gospel. This tireless Lutheran topographer has tramped every mile more than once and reports it in his *Following the Way. The Setting of John's Gospel* (Minneapolis: Augsburg, 1980), 223 pages. He may discourage some—and encourage others—by his seeming acceptance of the fourth gospel as a daybook of Jesus' journeys, but that noncritical view of history does nothing to cloud his critical faculties when it comes to geography and archaeology. This is a most informative book.

Jacob Jervell, the Norwegian scholar associated with Lucan studies, published in Oslo in 1978 a book that became in translation, *Jesus in the Gospel of John* (Minneapolis: Augsburg, 1984), 96 pages. It is excellent in every way, its summary of scholarly readings in particular, except for its assumption that the people of Israel somehow *in toto* rejected Jesus (pp. 64–65).

The much published exegete Peter Ellis produced *The Genius of John. A Composition-Critical History of the Fourth Gospel* (Collegeville, 1984), 230 pages. It is in verse-commentary form, popularizing the theory of John Gerhard, S.J. in his 1975 Catholic University of America dissertation, *The Literary Unity and the Compositional Methods of the Gospel of John,* that it is the work of one man (7:53—8:11 excepted); it was written according to the laws of chiastic parallelism, not the laws of narrative. Apart from the prologue—also chiastic in form—there are five parts and twenty-one sequences, varying in length from six verses to five chapters. Jesus' walking on the sea (6:16–21) is at the center of the gospel-length χ (*chi*). Corresponding words and phrases in the hypothetical parallel structure are identified by boldface type. Ellis' commentary is better than the hypothesis. With Judith Monahan Ellis he has published *John. An Access Guide for Scripture Study* (New York: W.H. Sadlier, 1983), 173 pages, which employs the above scheme of five parts and twenty-one sequences in parallel, but in an unobtrusive way.

Daniel Harrington, S.J. writes in his customary workmanlike fashion of the structure, purpose and key ideas of the FG in *John's Thought and Theology. An Introduction* (Wilmington, 1990), 120 pages, while William S. Kurz, S.J. examines Jn 13—17 among *The Farewell Addresses in the New Testament* (*idem*).

When it comes to prayerful treatments of Jn the landscape is far less well populated. Of the scholar-writers, Joseph A. Grassi in his articles and Paul S. Minear in his articles and one book on Jn have more "sap" of the Spirit than most.

Josef Blank, in *The Gospel according to St. John,* gen. ed. John L. McKenzie; 3 vols. (New York, 1981), derives his researches in Johannine christology and eschatology from his scholarly *Krisis* of 1964. The German series in which the shorter books appear is directed toward Christian prayer. Blank's volumes regularly divide pericopes into "exegesis" and "meditation" but the author is obviously ill at ease in the second part. This results in a useful but dull summary of exegetical findings throughout.

The largest success in this category comes from a Dutch Mill Hill Missionary based in England, John Wijngaards. His *The Gospel of John and His Letters,* Carolyn Osiek, ed., is volume 11 in the Message of Biblical Spirituality Series (Wilmington, 1986), 304 pages. The three sections of the book, in thirty brief chapters, are entitled Turning Towards the Light, The Father, and Abundance of

Life. The subheadings of the last section are: Inherited autonomy, Involvement and service, and Liberating dreams. The text is replete with poetic and other literary reference while the notes reflect acquaintance with a broad body of scholarship. The gospel is divided into "seven weeks—seven signs." This and other pedagogical devices may startle the fastidious but, all things considered, the book is an ingenious incentive to reflection and prayer.

Finally, the present writer's *John* (Atlanta, 1988), 276 pages, regularly attempts to go beyond the exegetical, with what success it is for the reader to say. On balance it must be maintained that no one has yet come up to the combination of scholarship and piety achieved by Sir Edwyn Hoskyns in his commentary of 1940.

Some Conclusions

Summarizing what they are saying about John in the last two decades is not easy because so much has been said. It would include an emerging consensus on the Hebraic character of the gospel despite its thin Hellenistic overlay, and the familiarity with Palestine of whoever provided its earliest formulation—in other words, its rootedness in the life of Jesus' disciples, of whom the one Jesus loved (if he is not John) and Peter are to the fore. Tracking Jn's relation to the synoptics is no longer a growth industry, while reconstructing the community that produced it, and by what stages, is. For this, the three epistles of John provide essential clues. The renewed awareness that Jn, like the other gospels, must be read as a proclamation of faith in Jesus Christ to the writer's or writers' believing contemporaries rather than a record of Jesus' words and deeds has prompted a reading of every line at two levels: "then" as a pointer to "now" and "now" as a clue to "then."

The search for written sources which the next to last writer, the evangelist, might have employed continues, but not with the earlier assurance that tradition and redaction is the way that Jn, like the synoptics, came to be. In the source question. Von Wahlde's separating of a later edition of the signs gospel from the earliest edition (marked by a low christology and relatively mild hostility to those who believe in Jesus otherwise and the authority figures who do not believe in him) promises to explain much.

"Jews" is used in the second edition for those most antagonistic to the ethnically Jewish Johannine community, and "works," not "signs," for his wonders. This would account for the bitter polemics and speech that have caused this "most Jewish of the gospels" (a designation from which Matthew is rapidly being dislodged) to be considered an "anti-Jewish gospel." The watershed of mutual antipathy might well have been the heightened christological claims which, in the editor's mind, brought on whatever sanction was represented by "out of the synagogue."

The most important contemporary development, perhaps, is the reading of John as the kind of literary product it is, a narrative or story, independently of historical considerations such as authorship and time, place, or circumstances of composition. In the literary exploration, exegesis of its texts is of more, not less, importance but always with a view to the story's plot and purpose: what the final editor of Jn hoped to convey in the realm of religion and faith, and how he framed the narrative he employed to do it. The gospel's symbolic speech is paramount here, for to put an overall historical construction on it is to read it falsely, whereas to discern the symbolism in which the story is clothed is to read it truly.

Notes

Introduction

1. Like the present writer's *John. A Commentary for Teachers and Preachers,* "Interpretation" (Atlanta, 1988). Similar titles are listed on pp. 91–96 below.

1. The Landmark Commentaries

1. See Arnold Ehrhardt, "The Gospels in the Muratorian Fragment" in *The Framework of the New Testament Stories* (Cambridge, 1964), p. 19, which provides the Latin text; full English text in Bruce Metzger, *The Canon of the New Testament: Its Origin, Development, and Significance* (Oxford, 1987), pp. 305–07.

2. *The History of the Church* 3.39.

3. Metzger, p. 55.

4. 1 *Apology,* 66.3; *Dialogue with Trypho,* 103.8.

5. 1 *Apol.* 46.2; *Dial.* 105.1.

6. 1 *Apol.* 61.4, an apparent quotation of Jn 3:3, 5.

7. *Dial.,* 81.4.

8. See Metzger, p. 150.

9. See Elaine Pagels, *The Johannine Gospel in Gnostic Exegesis. Heracleon's Commentary on John* (Nashville and New York, 1971), pp. 86–88.

10. *Adv. Haer.,* 3.1.1f., quoted in Eusebius, *H.C.,* 5.8.

11. Quoted in Eusebius, *H.C.* 6.14.7.

12. E.C. Hoskyns, ed. [posthumously by] F.N. Davey, *The Fourth Gospel* (London, 1940, 1947²).

13. Rudolf Bultmann, *The Gospel of John* (Göttingen, 1941; ET Philadelphia, 1971).

14. C.K. Barrett, *The Gospel According to St. John* (London, 1955; Philadelphia, 1978²).

15. C.H. Dodd, *The Interpretation of the Fourth Gospel* (Cambridge, 1953); *Historical Tradition in the Fourth Gospel* (Cambridge, 1963).

16. Rudolf Schnackenburg, *The Gospel According to John*, 3 vols. (Freiburg, 1965–75; ET New York, 1968–82).

17. Raymond E. Brown, *The Gospel According to John*, Doubleday Anchor Bible, 29 and 29A (Garden City, 1966–70).

18. F-M. Braun, *Jean le Théologien*, 2 vols. (Paris, 1959–64).

19. Barnabas Lindars, *The Gospel of John* (London, 1972).

20. Ernst Haenchen, *John*, 2 vols. (Tübingen, 1980; ET Philadelphia, 1984). The bibliography in vol. 2, 254–346, the work of translator-editor Robert W. Funk and editor Ulrich Busse, is superb.

21. Robert Kysar, *The Fourth Evangelist and His Gospel* (Minneapolis, 1975); "The Fourth Gospel. A Report on Recent Research," II/3, *Aufstieg und Niedergang der Römischer Welt*, ed. H. Temporini and W. Haase (Berlin, 1985), 2389–2480. Reviewed are more than 400 books and articles of 290 authors, the latest dated 1977. Another 66 authors in works published 1977–83 are listed in "The Gospel of John in Current Research," *Religious Studies Review*, 9/4 (Oct. 1983), 314–23. See also Edward Malatesta, *St. John's Gospel: 1920–1965* (Rome, 1967) and Hartwig Thyen, "Aus der Literatur zum Johannesevangelium," *Theologische Rundschau* 39 (1974) and 42 (1977).

22. Wilbert Francis Howard, *The Fourth Gospel in Recent Criticism and Interpretation* (rev. by C.K. Barrett; London, 1955).

23. See n. 1 above.

24. Hoskyns and Davey, p. 84.

25. *Idem*, p. 163.

26. *Idem*. p. 122.

27. Bultmann, 16; 17, n. 5.

28. P. 43; see also 47, 53, 81 for the self-understanding that man constantly seeks and that constantly eludes him except for the

absolute revelation in Jesus, which alone makes it possible to see himself as he is before God.

29. P. 67, n. 2; see also p. 83.

30. Kysar, 14.

31. Bultmann, 84–85.

32. *Idem*, 85.

33. *Idem*.

34. Bultmann, 111.

35. *Idem*, 461.

36. A. Faure, "Die alttestamentliche Zitate in 4. Evangelium und Quellenscheidungshypothese," *Zeitschrift für die neutestamentliche Wissenschaft*, 21 (1922), 107ff.

37. Kysar, 26–27. The authors are R. Schnackenburg, *op. cit.*; Jürgen Becker, "Wunder und Christologie," *New Testament Studies*, 16 (1969–70), 130–48; Robert T. Fortna, *The Gospel of Signs. A Reconstruction of the Narrative Source Underlying the Fourth Gospel* (Cambridge, 1970); W. Nicol, *The Sēmeia in the Fourth Gospel* (Brill, 1972); Howard M. Teeple, *The Literary Origin of the Gospel of John* (Evanston, 1974).

38. See Bultmann, 111. The translator of this book, George R. Beasley-Murray, has produced an exhaustive commentary of his own of high quality, *John*, 36 "Word Biblical Commentary" (Waco, 1987).

39. (London, 1955; 1978²).

40. Barrett, 1978², 26.

41. *Idem*, 40.

42. *Idem*, 39.

43. *Idem*, 74.

44. *Idem*, 89, 91.

45. See *idem*, 583–87.

46. *Idem*, 120; in *The Gospel of John and Judaism* (Philadelphia, 1975), the Franz Delitzsch Lectures written in German and translated by D.M. Smith, Barrett concluded that Jn combines gnosis and anti-gnosticism, apocalyptic and non-apocalyptic material, Judaism and anti-Judaism, all in a theological synthesis based on a dialectic between love and *gnōsis,* in the historical situation in which John finds himself.

47. See n. 15 above.
48. *Idem.*
49. Dodd, *Interpretation,* pp. 444–53.
50. *Ibid.,* p. 445.
51. Dodd, *Historical Tradition,* pp. 348, 349.
52. *Ibid.,* pp. 424–25.
53. *Ibid.,* p. 426.
54. *Ibid.,* p. 150. On pp. 28–30 he provides such a *schema,* opting against a literary dependence of Jn and in favor of "all four evangelists [having] felt themselves to be bound by a pre-canonical tradition in which the broad lines of the story were already fixed" (p. 30).
55. *Ibid.,* p. 115. Such is the conclusion of a number of contemporary scholars who question whether the total non-implication of Jesus in the political events in Roman Palestine, as reported by the evangelists, can have been true to the facts.
56. P. 123.
57. P. 172.
58. P. 194.
59. P. 232.
60. P. 300.
61. Pp. 386–87.
62. P. 420.
63. P. 128.
64. *Ibid.*
65. See Paul Achtemeier, *"Omne Verbum Sonat:* The New Testament and the Oral Environment of Late Western Antiquity," *Journal of Biblical Literature* 109, 1 (March 1990), 3–27.
66. Brown, *The Gospel According to John (xiii–xxi)* (Garden City, NY: Doubleday Anchor Bible 29A, 1970), 1080–82.
67. Brown, *idem* 29, p. C.
68. *Ibid.*
69. *Ibid.,* p. CI.
70. *Ibid.,* p. 23.
71. *Ibid.,* p. LXXI.
72. *Ibid.,* p. LXXII.
73. *Ibid.,* p. LXXIV.
74. See *ibid.,* p. 374, n. 22. By Vol. 29A, 691 this has been

modified to Jn's "referring to the Synagogue in general and fighting a policy that is, at least, in effect in all the synagogues of the area he knows."

75. See, for example, his positing of four independent sources for Jn 20:10, resulting in vv. 1–2, 3–10; 11:13; 14–18 (which had two other independent forms, Mk 10:9–11 and Mt 28:9–10), in *John* (*xii–xxi*) 29A, 998–1004.

76. See n. 16 above; the three volumes cover a little over 1,700 pages.

77. Schnackenburg, I, 46–47.

78. *Ibid.*, p. 47.

79. *Ibid.*, p. 43.

80. *Ibid.*, pp. 101–04.

2. The Question of Sources

1. Eugen Ruckstuhl, *Die literarische Einheit des Johannesevangeliums* (Fribourg/Schweiz, 1951). Eduard Schweizer, *Egō Eimi* (Göttingen, 1939), had held a similar position on its stylistic unity, which he modified somewhat in a second edition (1965).

2. Wilhelm Wilkens, *Die Entstehung des vierten Evangeliums* (Zollikon, 1958); he has not departed from his original position in *Zeichen und Werke* (Zürich, 1969). Later studies in tradition and redaction were done by W. Nicol of South Africa, *The Sēmeia in the Fourth Gospel* (Leiden, 1972) and Howard M. Teeple, *The Literary Origin of the Gospel of John* (Evanston, 1974). Using form analysis Nicol showed how the miracle stories in the signs source are to be separated out from Jn. Teeple posited a signs source (SA) and a semi-gnostic, Hellenistic mysticism source, mostly of discourses (G). These were edited into a gospel by the evangelist (E) whose work was subsequently recast by a redactor (R).

3. D. Moody Smith, *The Composition and Order of the Fourth Gospel: Bultmann's Literary Theory* (New Haven and London, 1965).

4. Robert Tomson Fortna, *The Gospel of Signs. A Reconstruction of the Narrative Source Underlying the Fourth Gospel* (Cambridge, England, 1970).

5. *Ibid.,* p. 2.
6. *Ibid.,* p. 217.
7. See p. 223.
8. See p. 225.
9. Robert Tomson Fortna, *The Fourth Gospel and Its Predecessor. From Narrative Source to Present Gospel* (Philadelphia, 1988).
10. *Ibid.,* p. 35, n. 61.
11. Urban C. von Wahlde, *The Earliest Version of John's Gospel. Recovering the Gospel of Signs* (Wilmington, 1989).
12. *Ibid.,* Appendix A, pp. 190–91, where they are listed. In Ch. 3, pp. 66–155, they are scrutinized and defended.
13. M.C. White, *The Identity and Function of Jews and Related Terms in the Fourth Gospel* (Ann Arbor, microfilm, 1972).
14. Von Wahlde cites Brown, p. 526, as holding this view, with 7:3 as an exception.
15. Von Wahlde, p. 174.
16. P. 57.
17. P. 47, n. 53.
18. His extended n. 136 on pp. 134–35 is important in this regard. Unlike most who look for a source behind the passion material, von Wahlde has no recourse to comparison with the synoptics but uses his earlier criteria: "Pharisees" once, "chief priests" throughout, "Jews" as Judeans only, concept and place names in Aramaic and Greek in the two reverse orders, and no theological development beyond Jesus as "the Christ, the Son of God" (20:31).
19. D. Moody Smith, *Johannine Christianity. Essays on Its Setting, Sources and Theology* (Columbia, 1984), pp. 1–36.
20. These he had gone into in more detail in a paper of 1964, "The Sources of the Gospel of John," Chapter 1.
21. *Ibid.,* p. 16.
22. *Ibid.,* p. 24; but see his earlier recording of resistance to the idea, p. 81.
23. "Divine man," a Hellenistic model that is a construct of twentieth scholarship and has been called into question as a reality of the ancient world on the confident terms with which it is em-

ployed in New Testament studies. Smith calls the existence "of such a christology in some sense native to Judaism," widely regarded as well established, "The Johannine Miracle Source" (1967), *ibid.*, pp. 65, 67.

24. Smith, p. 35.
25. *Ibid.*, "The Sources," p. 60.
26. *Ibid.*, p. 76.
27. *Catholic Biblical Quarterly* 51, 1 (Jan. 1989), 147.
28. Wolfgang J. Bittner, *Jesu Zeichen in Johannesevangelium* (Tübingen, 1987).
29. *History and Theology in the Fourth Gospel* (New York, 1968); 2nd rev. ed. (Nashville, 1979). See also some learned papers in reprint: *The Gospel of John in Recent History. Essays for Interpreters* (New York, 1978).
30. "Glimpses into the History of the Johannine Community. From Its Origin through the Period of Its Life in Which the Fourth Gospel Was Composed," in Marinus de Jonge, ed., *L'Evangile de Jean. Sources, Réduction, Théologie* (Gembloux/Leuven, 1977), pp. 149–75.
31. *Ibid.*, p. 158.
32. P. 163.
33. *The Gospel of John* (London, 1972).
34. *Behind the Fourth Gospel* (London, 1971).
35. "Traditions behind the Fourth Gospel" in *L'Evangile de Jean*, ed. M. de Jonge, pp. 107–24.
36. *Ibid.*, p. 107.
37. Lindars, *Behind*, p. 47.
38. (London, 1976; German original, 1975), pp. 9–10, 98.
39. John A.T. Robinson, *The Priority of John*, ed. by J.F. Coakley (London, 1985).
40. *Ibid.*, p. 5.
41. P. 9.
42. Pp. 20–21, quoting Kysar, p. 24.
43. Robinson, p. 67; elsewhere in a footnote he reports the unhappiness of A.J.B. Higgins and James Montgomery at calling it "the Fourth Gospel" (for the latter, a "scholastic affectation"), although Robinson employs the term throughout. See p. 4, n. 6.

44. (London, 1976).

45. Robinson, *TPOJ*, p. 67, n. 150 summarizing his argument in Ch. IX of *RTNT* (254–311).

46. *Ibid.*, pp. 23–24

47. See p. 24.

48. P. 26.

49. *Ibid.*

50. P. 8.

51. P. 4.

52. P. 5.

53. Review in *JBL*, 108, 1 (Spring 1989), 156–58.

54. Cullmann, *op. cit.*, p. 49.

55. See John Bowman, *The Fourth Gospel and the Jews* (Pittsburgh, 1975) for an explanation of this agricultural proverb (p. 114).

56. "Samaria and the Origins of the Christian Mission," *The Early Church* (London, 1956). Barrett, *op. cit.*, p. 243, n. 38, thinks the opinion wrong. See Raymond E. Brown, *The Community of the Beloved Disciple* (New York, 1979) for the suggestion that Jn 4 is a turning point in the gospel for the "entrance into Johannine Christianity of another group which catalyzed the christological developments [viz., toward an increasingly 'higher' Johannine christology]," p. 34. On Brown's *Community,* see further on pp. 63–64 below.

57. *The Johannine School* (Missoula, 1974).

58. *Ibid.*, pp. 258–59.

59. Pp. 287–89.

60. P. 269.

61. (Philadelphia, 1990).

62. P. 130.

63. P. 131.

64. P. 103.

65. P. 105; cf. pp. 72–73.

66. See pp. 114–19 with n. 52, p. 213. Besides the articles cited there, of P. Schäfer (*Judaica*, 1975), G. Stemberger (*Kairos*, 1977), R. Kimelman (*JTS* NS, 1982) and S.I. Katz (*JBL*, 1984), see Kimelman's shorter, "*Birkat Ha-Minim* and the Lack of Evidence for an Anti-Christian Jewish Prayer in Late Antiquity," in

E.P. Sanders *et al.*, eds., *Jewish and Christian Self-Definition*, Vol. Two, *Aspects of Judaism in the Greco-Roman Period* (Philadelphia, 1981), pp. 226–44.

3. John as Religious Literature

1. Klaus Koch, *The Growth of the Biblical Tradition: The Form-Critical Method* (New York, 1969), p. 69.

2. Norman R. Petersen, *Literary Criticism for New Testament Critics* (Philadelphia, 1978). The first part of this short book is on Mark's gospel, the second, less successful part on a Lucan question. See also David Rhoads and Donald Michie, *Mark as Story. An Introduction to the Narrative of a Gospel* (Philadelphia, 1982).

3. Frank Kermode, *The Genesis of Secrecy. On the Interpretation of Narrative* (Cambridge, 1979); Northrop Frye, *The Great Code: The Bible and Literature* (New York and London, 1982)— prompting irreverent thoughts of a title such as *Shakespeare and Literature*.

4. *The Literary Devices in John's Gospel* (1970).

5. R. Alan Culpepper, *Anatomy of the Fourth Gospel. A Study in Literary Design* (Philadelphia, 1983).

6. Jack Dean Kingsbury, *Matthew as Story* (Philadelphia, 1986).

7. Culpepper, *Anatomy*, p. 231.

8. P. 232, Culpepper received some sharp criticism from Jeffrey Lloyd Staley in *The Print's First Kiss. A Rhetorical Investigation of the Implied Reader in the Fourth Gospel* (Atlanta, 1988) for his inaccurate use of terms such as narrator, implied author, and implied reader as if they were firmly fixed. The pun of Staley's title indicates that he is concerned with the impact made on the reader by a text prepared for oral delivery, but later captured first in manuscripts (a fluid medium), then print. That done, he examines the prologue followed by chs. 1—3 and five later passages where the narrator seems self-contradictory but has consciously planted tensions for the reader to embrace.

9. P. 234.

10. Pp. 48–49.

11. P. 35.
12. P. 41.
13. Pp. 43–48.
14. Culpepper, p. 88.
15. *Irony in the Fourth Gospel* (Atlanta, 1985).
16. P. 151.
17. *Revelation in the Fourth Gospel. Narrative Mode and Theological Claim* (Philadelphia, 1986).
18. P. 26, quoting D.C. Muecke, "Irony Markers," *Poetics* 7 (1968): 365. O'Day cites favorably George W. MacRae, S.J., "Theology and Irony in the Fourth Gospel," in *The Word and the World. Essays in Honor of F.L. Moriarty,* ed. R.J. Clifford (Cambridge, 1973), pp. 83–96.
19. P. 113 citing Amos N. Wilder's *Theopoetic. Theology and the Religious Imagination* (Philadelphia, 1976), p. 92.
20. *Ibid.*
21. Godfrey C. Nicholson, *Death as Departure: The Johannine Descent-Ascent Schema* (Chico, 1983). Ernst Käsemann gave the Shaffer Lecture at Yale in 1966, published later that same year in German (Tübingen) but in English as *The Testament of Jesus. A Study of the Gospel of John in the Light of Chapter 17* (Philadelphia, 1968). He saw in this chapter the literary convention of the biblical address of a dying man, corresponding to the prologue and effectively bringing the gospel to a close. It showed the whole gospel to be a piece of "naïve docetism" in which the author "spiritualized old apocalyptic traditions." The church accepted into its canon through human error and God's providence this presentation of "Jesus as God walking the face of the earth" (p. 75), a "dangerous theology" that nonetheless "calls us into our creatureliness" and shows us "the one final testament of the earthly Jesus and his glory" (p. 78).
22. P. 166.
23. (Philadelphia, 1988).
24. P. 128.
25. (Philadelphia, 1988).
26. See pp. 28–29.
27. P. 60.
28. See p. 61.

29. In doing so he sides with Martyn, *HTFG*² (pp. 87–88) but does not see in Nicodemus' anointing of Jesus' body (against Brown, Schnackenburg and Lindars) a gesture of devotion, even confession (pp. 38–40). Jouette Bassler finds Jn leaving Nicodemus a completely ambiguous figure in the three places where he appears (3:1–21; 71:45–52; 19:38–42) as part of a cognitive "gap" intended by the author, forcing the reader to wrestle with the contours of Johannine faith. See, "Mixed Signals: Nicodemus in the Fourth Gospel" *JBL* 108, 4 (Winter 1989) 635–46.

30. See p. 74.

31. See pp. 78–79, 110–11; cf. Frederick Herzog, *Liberation in the Light of the Fourth Gospel* (New York, 1972), which Rensberger thinks not without value, but, on balance, a disappointment because of its neglect of exegesis. A Salamanca dissertation that explores Jn 7:1—10:21 is Hugo C. Zorilla's *La fiesta de liberación de los oprimidos,* whose conclusions are summarized in *Mission Focus* 13 (1985) 21–24.

32. Rensberger, 114.

33. Wayne A. Meeks, "The Man from Heaven in Johannine Sectarianism," JBL 91 (1972) 44–72; cf. Marinus de Jonge, "Nicodemus and Jesus" in *Jesus: Stranger from Heaven and Son of God* (Missoula, 1974) 29–48, who sees Nicodemus' sympathy and incorrect faith in Jesus as set in opposition to Johannine faith.

34. Rensberger, 136.

35. Jerome H. Neyrey, S.J., *An Ideology of Revolt. John's Christology in Social Science Perspective* (Philadelphia, 1988). For the remarks on point of view, see pp. 97 and 239, n. 8.

36. Neyrey, 33.

37. *Ibid.*

38. P. 35.

39. P. 58.

40. P. 92.

41. Pp. 117–18; a fourth or final stage is "represented by ch. 21 and the moderation of earlier spiritualist tendencies (see 1 and 2 John as well)."

42. P. 127.

43. P. 147.

44. (New York, 1979). See also D. Bruce Woll, *Johannine*

Christianity in Conflict. Authority, Rank, and Succession in the First Farewell Discourses (Chico, 1989).
45. *The Epistles of John* (Garden City, 1982). A previous work on the longest of these was John Bogart's *Orthodox and Heretical Perfectionism in the Johannine Community as Evident in the First Epistle of John* (Missoula, 1977).
46. *The New Testament World. Insights from Cultural Anthropology* (Atlanta, 1981); later, *Christian Origins and Cultural Anthropology. Practical Models for Biblical Interpretation* (*idem*, 1986). Douglas' first book-length presentation of group and grid was in *Natural Symbols* (New York, 1982).
47. P. 170.
48. P. 143.
49. *The Testament of Jesus. A Study of the Gospel of John in the Light of Chapter 17* (Philadelphia, 1968).
50. Teresa Okure, R.H.C.J., *The Johannine Approach to Mission. A Contextual Study of John 4:1–42* (Tübingen, 1988).
51. Pp. 50–51.
52. For the historical probabilities underlying the story of Jn 4, see pp. 188–91.
53. Pp. 187–88.

4. Treatments of Johannine Themes

1. Gary M. Burge, *The Anointed Community. The Holy Spirit in the Johannine Tradition* (Grand Rapids, 1987).
2. Burge, p. 41.
3. Felix Porsch, C.S.Sp., *Pneuma und Wort. Ein exegetischer Beitrag zur Pneumatologie des Johannesevangeliums* (Frankfurt, 1974). Review by D. M. Smith, *JBL* 96, 3 (Sept. 1977), 458–59. From this Gregorian University dissertation came a shorter study, *Anwalt der Glaubenden. Das wirken des Geistes nach dem Zeugnis Johannesevangelium* (Stuttgart, 1978).
4. Ignace de la Potterie, S.J., *La Vérité dans S. Jean*, 2 vols. (Rome, 1977). Burge refers particularly to his Chapter 5, "Le Paraclet, l'Esprit de la Vérité."
5. Burge, p. 43.
6. *Ibid.*

7. P. 49.
8. See p. 81.
9. Pp. 83, 84.
10. See pp. 85; 87.
11. P. 100.
12. See pp. 148–49.
13. P. 193.
14. Pp. 220–21.
15. Woll, p. 63.
16. P. 127.
17. Severino Pancaro, *The Law in the Fourth Gospel. The Torah and the Gospel, Moses and Jesus, Judaism and Christianity according to John* (Leiden, 1975).
18. Pp. 510–11.
19. Anthony Ernest Harvey, *Jesus on Trial. A Study in the Fourth Gospel* (London, 1976; Atlanta, 1977).
20. P. 130.
21. See p. 131.
22. P. 55.
23. See p. 5.
24. See p. 57.
25. See p. 55.
26. *Christology in Paul and John* (Philadelphia, 1988). Part 2, "The Christology of John," pp. 53–102.
27. Pp. 80–84.
28. P. 83. Meeks's "Man from Heaven" is cited here. See n. 33, p. 109 above. He further observes (p. 84) that "The use of irony may be humorous for insiders, but it wins no debates with outsiders."
29. P. 102.
30. J. Terence Forestell, C.S.B., *The Word of the Cross. Salvation as Revelation in the Fourth Gospel* (Rome, 1974).
31. Francis J. Moloney, S.D.B., *The Johannine Son of Man* (Rome, 1976).
32. Forestell, p. 16.
33. Barnabas Lindars, SSF, *Jesus Son of Man. A Fresh Examination of the Son of Man Sayings in the Gospels in the Light of Recent Research* (Grand Rapids, 1984). The quotation is on p. 155.

Lindars agrees with Moloney that the use of Son of Man in 5:27 is titular and there it *may* be connected with Dan 7:13–14—of which Jn should not be presumed ignorant. But even in that case it refers to the one whose crucifixion bespeaks God's glory. Interestingly, Lindars does not cite Forestell in his brief chapter on Jn (pp. 145–57) while largely coming to the same conclusion as he on what Son of Man means for this evangelist.

34. *Structure and Meaning in the Fourth Gospel. A Text-Linguistic Analysis of John 2:1–11 and 4:1–42,* tr. J. Gray (Lund, 1974).

35. *The Epistles of John Translated with Introduction, Notes and Commentary.* Doubleday Anchor Bible 30 (Garden City, 1982). In 1973 there had appeared a translation of Rudolf Bultmann's *The Johannine Epistles* in the Hermeneia commentary (Philadelphia, 1973; Göttingen, 1967²), and more recently Urban C. von Wahlde's *The Johannine Commandments. 1 John and the Struggle for the Johannine Tradition* (Mahwah, 1990). The latter builds on Brown to show that the opponents of 1 Jn in their interpretation of the Johannine commandments have one-sidedly exaggerated the role of the Spirit and underplayed that of Jesus.

36. Mark Kiley may be closer to the mark in "The Exegesis of God: Jesus' Signs in John 1–11," *SBL 1988 Seminar Papers* (Atlanta: Scholars, 1988), 555–69 in correlating six of Jn's minor signs (i.e. exclusive of cross-resurrection) with passages in Ps 23 and the seventh, the man blind from birth, with Ps 27.

37. J. Leal, "El Simbolismo historico del IV evangelio," *Estudios Biblicos* 19 (1960), 329–48; X. Léon-Dufour, "Towards a Symbolic Understanding of the Fourth Gospel," *NTS* 27 (1981) 439–56.

Some Commentaries

Barrett, Charles Kingsley, *The Gospel According to St. John* (London: S.P.C.K., 1955; 2d rev. ed., Philadelphia: Westminster, 1978).

Beasley-Murray, George Raymond, *John*, 36 ("Word Biblical Commentary"; Waco: Word, 1987).

Becker, Jürgen, *Das Evangelium des Johannes* (2 vols.; Gütersloh; Gerd Mohn, 1979–81).

Bernard, John Henry, *The Gospel According to St. John* (2 vols.; New York: Scribner's, 1929).

Braun, François-Marie, *L'Évangile selon Saint Jean* ("La Sainte Bible"; Paris: Letouzey et Ané, 1946).

Brown, Raymond Edward, *The Gospel According to John* (Garden City: Doubleday Anchor Bible 29 and 29A, 1966, 1970).

————. *The Epistles of John*, DAB 30 (*idem*, 1982).

————. *The Gospel and Epistles of John. A Concise Commentary* (Collegeville: Liturgical, 1988).

Bultmann, Rudolf, *The Gospel of John* (Philadelphia: Westminster, 1971; German orig., Göttingen: Vanderhoeck u. Ruprecht, 1941).

————. *The Johannine Epistles,* "Hermeneia" (Philadelphia: Fortress, 1973; German, 1967[2]).

Carson, D.A., *The Gospel According to John* (Grand Rapids: Eerdmans, 1991).

Ellis, Peter, *The Genius of John. A Composition-Critical Commentary on the Fourth Gospel* (Collegeville: Liturgical, 1984).

Haenchen, Ernst, *John 1* and *John 2* ("Hermeneia"; Philadelphia: Fortress, 1984; German orig., Tübingen: Siebeck [Mohr], 1980).

Hoskyns, Edwyn Clement and Francis Noel Davey, *The Fourth Gospel* (London: Faber and Faber, 1940; 2d ed. 1947).

Kysar, Robert, *John* ("Augsburg Commentaries on the New Testament"; Minneapolis: Augsburg, 1987).

Lindars, Barnabas, *The Gospel of John* ("New Century Bible"; Grand Rapids: Eerdmans, 1972).

Morris, Leon, *The Gospel According to John* ("The New International Critical Commentary"; Grand Rapids: Eerdmans, 1971).

Perkins, Pheme, *The Gospel According to St. John. A Theological Commentary* (Chicago: Franciscan Herald, 1978).

————. "John," in *The New Jerome Biblical Commentary* (Englewood Cliffs: Prentice-Hall, 1989), Ch. 61, pp. 942–85.

Sanders, Joseph Newbold and B.A. Mastin, *The Gospel According to St. John* ("Harper's New Testament Commentaries Series"; Peabody: Hendrickson, 1987; first pub., London: A. and C. Black, 1968).

Schlatter, Adolf, *Der Evangelist Johannes* (Stuttgart: Calwer, 1975⁴).

Schnackenburg, Rudolf, *The Gospel According to John* (3 vols.; New York: Crossroad, 1968–82; German orig., Freiburg: Herder, 1965–75).

Sloyan, Gerard Stephen, *John* ("Interpretation Series: A Biblical Commentary for Teaching and Preaching"; Atlanta: John Knox, 1988).

Smith, Dwight Moody, "John," in *Harper's Bible Commentary* (San Francisco: Harper and Row, 1988), pp. 1044–76.

Some Further Reading

Achtemeier, Paul, "*Omne Verbum Sonat:* The New Testament and the Oral Environment of Late Western Antiquity," *Journal of Biblical Literature* 109, 1 (March 1990), 3–27.

Auerbach, Erich, *Mimesis. The Representation of Reality in Western Literature* (Princeton: Princeton University, 1953).

Barrett, C.K., *The Gospel of John and Judaism* (Philadelphia: Westminster, 1975).

Bassler, Jouette, "The Galileans: A Neglected Factor in Johannine Community Research," *Catholic Biblical Quarterly* 43, 2 (April 1981), 243–57.

————. "Mixed Signals: Nicodemus in the Fourth Gospel," *Journal of Biblical Literature* 108, 4 (Winter 1989), 635–46.

Bittner, Wolfgang J., *Jesu Zeichen in Johannesevangelium* (Tübingen: Mohr [Siebeck], 1987).

Bogart, John, *Orthodox and Heretical Perfectionism in the Johannine Community as Evident in the First Epistle of John* (Missoula: Scholars, 1977).

Botha, J.E., "Reader 'Entrapment' as Literary Device in John 4: 1–42," *Neotestamentica* (South Africa) 24, 1 (1990), 37–47.

Bowman, John, *The Fourth Gospel and the Jews* (Pittsburgh: Pickwick, 1975).

Braun, F.-M., *Jean le Théologien et son évangile dans l'église ancienne* (2 vols.; Paris: J. Gabalda, 1959–64).

Brown, Raymond E. *The Community of the Beloved Disciple* (New York: Paulist, 1979).

Burge, Gary M., *The Anointed Community. The Holy Spirit in the Johannine Tradition* (Grand Rapids: Eerdmans, 1987).

Charlesworth, James H., ed., *John and the Dead Sea Scrolls* (2d rev. ed.; New York: Crossroad, 1990).

Cullmann, Oscar, *The Johannine Circle* (Philadelphia: Westminster, 1976; German orig., 1975).

_____. "Samaria and the Origins of the Christian Mission," *The Early Church* (London: SCM, 1956).

Culpepper, R. Alan, *The Johannine School. An Investigation . . . Based on the Nature of Ancient Schools* (Missoula: Scholars, 1975).

_____. *Anatomy of the Fourth Gospel. A Study in Literary Design* (Philadelphia: Fortress, 1983).

Dodd, C.H., *The Interpretation of the Fourth Gospel* (Cambridge: Cambridge University, 1953).

_____. *Historical Tradition in the Fourth Gospel* (*idem*, 1963).

Douglas, Mary, *Purity and Danger. An Analysis of Concepts of Pollution and Taboo* (London: Routledge and Kegan Paul, 1966, 1969²).

————. *Natural Symbols. Exploration in Cosmology* (New York: Pantheon, 1982).

Duke, Paul D., *Irony in the Fourth Gospel* (Atlanta: John Knox, 1985).

Ehrhardt, Arnold, *The Framework of the New Testament Stories* (Cambridge: Cambridge University, 1964).

Eusebius, *The Ecclesiastical History,* tr. by Kirsopp Lake (2 vols.; Cambridge: Harvard University, 1926, 1932); *The History of the Church from Christ to Constantine,* tr. by G.A. Williamson (Harmondsworth: Penguin, 1965).

Faure, Alexander, "Die alttestamentlichen Zitate im 4. Evangelium und die Quellenscheidungshypothese," *Zeitschrift für die neutestamentliche Wissenschaft* 21 (1922), 99–121.

Forestell, J. Terence, *The Word of the Cross. Salvation as Revelation in the Fourth Gospel* (Rome: Pontifical Biblical Institute, 1974).

Fortna, Robert T., *The Gospel of Signs. A Reconstruction of the Narrative Source Underlying the Fourth Gospel* (New York and London: Cambridge University, 1970).

————. *The Fourth Gospel and Its Predecessor. From Narrative Source to Present Gospel* (Philadelphia: Fortress, 1988).

Girard, Marc, "La composition structurelle des sept signes dans le quatrième évangile," *Studies in Religion / Sciences Religieuses* 9, 3 (1980), 315–24.

Glasson, Thomas F., *Moses in the Fourth Gospel* (Naperville, IL: A.R. Allenson, 1963).

Green-Armytage, A.H.N., *John Who Saw* (London: Faber and Faber, 1952).

Harrington, Daniel, *John's Thought and Theology. An Introduction* (Wilmington: Michael Glazier, 1990).

Harvey, A.E., *Jesus on Trial. A Study in the Fourth Gospel* (Atlanta: John Knox, 1977).

Herzog, Frederick. *Liberation Theology: Liberation in the Light of the Fourth Gospel* (New York: Seabury, 1972).

Howard, W.F., *The Fourth Gospel in Recent Criticism and Interpretation* (rev. by C.K. Barrett; London: Epworth, 1955).

Jonge, Marinus de, ed., *L'Evangile de Jean. Sources, Rédaction, Théologie* (Gembloux, Duculot; Leuven, University Press, 1977).

_____. *Jesus: Stranger from Heaven and Son of God* (Missoula: Scholars, 1977).

Karris, Robert, *Jesus and the Marginalized in John's Gospel* (Collegeville, MN: Michael Glazier/Liturgical, 1990).

Käsemann, Ernst, *The Testament of Jesus. A Study of the Gospel of John in the Light of Chapter 17* (Philadelphia: Fortress, 1968; German orig., 1966).

Katz, Steven T., "Issues in the Separation of Judaism and Christianity after 70 C.E.: A Reconsideration," *JBL* 103/1 (1984), 43–76.

Kermode, Frank, *The Genesis of Secrecy. On the Interpretation of Narrative* (Cambridge: Harvard University, 1979).

Kiley, Mark, "The Exegesis of God: Jesus' Signs in John 1–11," *SBL Seminar Papers* (Atlanta: Scholars, 1988), 555–69.

Kimelman, Reuven, "Birkat Ha-Minim and the Lack of Evidence for a Jewish Anti-Christian Prayer in Late Antiquity," in E.P.

Sanders, *et al.*, eds., *Jewish and Christian Self-Definition,* Vol. 2, *Aspects of Judaism in the Greco-Roman Period* (Philadelphia: Fortress, 1981), pp. 226–44.

Koch, Klaus, *The Growth of the Biblical Tradition, The Form-Critical Method* (New York: Scribner's, 1969).

Kurz, William S., *The Farewell Addresses in the New Testament* (Wilmington: Michael Glazier, 1990).

Kysar, Robert, *The Fourth Evangelist and His Gospel* (Minneapolis: Augsburg, 1975).

———. *John, The Maverick Gospel* (Atlanta: John Knox, 1976).

———. "The Gospel of John in Current Research," *Religious Studies Review,* 9/4 (Oct., 1983), 314–23.

———. *John's Story of Jesus* (Philadelphia: Fortress, 1984).

———. "The Fourth Gospel. A Report on Recent Research," II/3, *Aufstieg und Niedergang der Römischer Welt,* ed. H. Temporini and W. Haase (Berlin: de Gruyter, 1985), 2389–2480.

Leal, J., "El Simbolismo historico del IV evangelio," *Estudios Biblicos* 19 (1960), 329–48.

Léon-Dufour, X., "Towards a Symbolic Understanding of the Fourth Gospel," *NTS* 27 (1981), 439–56.

Lindars, Barnabas, *Jesus Son of Man. A Fresh Examination of the Son of Man Sayings in the Gospels . . .* (Grand Rapids: Eerdmans, 1984).

MacRae, George W., "Theology and Irony in the Fourth Gospel," in *The Word and the World,* ed. R.J. Clifford (Cambridge, MA: Weston College, 1973).

———. "The Fourth Gospel and Religionsgeschichte," *CBQ* 32, 1 (Jan., 1970), 13–24.

Malatesta, Edward, *St. John's Gospel*: 1920–1965 (Rome: Pontifical Biblical Institute, 1967).

Malina, Bruce, *The New Testament World. Insights from Cultural Anthropology* (Atlanta: John Knox, 1981).

———. *Christian Origins and Cultural Anthropology (idem,* 1986).

Martyn, J. Louis, *History and Theology in the Fourth Gospel* (2d rev. ed.; Nashville: Abingdon, 1979).

———. "Glimpses into the History of the Johannine Community," in Marinus de Jonge, ed., *L'Evangile de Jean. Sources, Rédaction, Théologie* (Gembloux/Leuven, 1977).

———. *The Gospel of John in Recent History* (New York: Paulist, 1978).

Meeks, Wayne A., *The Prophet-King. Moses Traditions and the Johannine Christology* (Leiden: E.J. Brill, 1967).

———. "The Man from Heaven in Johannine Sectarianism, *JBL* 91 (1972), 44–72.

Metzger, Bruce, *The Canon of the New Testament: Its Origin, Development, and Significance* (Oxford: Clarendon, 1987).

Minear, Paul, *John. The Martyr's Gospel* (New York: Pilgrim, 1984).

Moloney, Francis, *The Johannine Son of Man* (2d ed.; Rome: Ateneo Salesiano, 1979).

Morris, Leon, *Jesus Is the Christ. Studies in the Theology of John* (Grand Rapids: Eerdmans, 1971).

Neyrey, Jerome, *An Ideology of Revolt. John's Christology in So-cial Science Perspective* (Philadelphia: Fortress, 1988).

Nicholson, Godfrey C., *Death as Departure. The Johannine De-scent-Ascent Schema* (Chico: Scholars, 1983).

Nicol, W., *The Sēmeia in the Fourth Gospel. Tradition and Redac-tion* (Leiden: Brill, 1972).

O'Day, Gail, *Revelation in the Fourth Gospel. Narrative Mode and Theological Claim* (Philadelphia: Fortress, 1986).

Okure, Teresa, *The Johannine Approach to Mission. A Contextual Study of John 4:1–42* (Tübingen: Mohr [Siebeck], 1988).

Olsson, Birger, *Structure and Meaning in the Fourth Gospel. A Text-Linguistic Analysis of John 2:1–11 and 4:1–42* (Lund: Gleerup, 1974).

Pagels, Elaine, *The Johannine Gospel in Gnostic Exegesis. Hera-cleon's Commentary on John* (Missoula: Scholars, 1973).

Pancaro, Severino, *The Law in the Fourth Gospel. The Torah and the Gospel, Moses and Jesus, Judaism and Christianity Accord-ing to John* (Leiden: Brill, 1975).

Petersen, Norman R., *Literary Criticism for New Testament Critics* (Philadelphia: Fortress, 1978).

Porsch, Felix, *Pneuma und Wort. Ein exegetische Beitrag zur Pneumatologie des Johannesevangeliums* (Frankfurt: Josef Knecht, 1974).

Potterie, I. de la, *La Vérité dans S. Jean* (2 vols.; Rome: Pontifical Biblical Institute, 1977).

————. *The Hour of Jesus. The Passion and the Resurrection of Jesus According to John* (New York: Alba House, 1989).

Reitzenstein, Richard, *Das mandäische Buch des Herrn der Grösse und die Evangelien* (Heidelberg: Carl Winter, 1919).

Rensberger, David, *Johannine Faith and Liberating Community* (Philadelphia: Westminster, 1988).

Rhoads, David and Donald Michie, *Mark as Story* (Philadelphia: Fortress, 1982).

Richter, Georg, *Studien zum Johannesevangelium,* Herausgegeben von Josef Hainz (Regensburg: Friedrich Pustet, 1977).

Robinson, John A.T., *The Priority of John*, ed. by J.F. Coakley (London: SCM, 1985).

Ruckstuhl, Eugen, *Die literarische Einheit des Johannesevangeliums* (Freiburg/Schweiz: Paulus, 1951).

Sanders, E.P. *et al.*, eds., *Jewish and Christian Self-Definition*, Vol. 2, *Aspects of Judaism in the Greco-Roman Period* (Philadelphia: Fortress, 1981).

Schein, Bruce E., *Following in the Way. The Setting of John's Gospel* (Minneapolis: Augsburg, 1980).

Schweizer, Eduard, *Egō Eimi. Die religionsgeschictliche Herkunft . . . der johanneischen Bildreden . . .* (2d ed., Göttingen: Vandenhoeck und Ruprecht, 1965).

Scroggs, Robin, *Christology in John and Paul* (Philadelphia: Fortress, 1988).

Segovia, Fernando F., *Love Relationships in the Fourth Gospel* (Atlanta: John Knox, 1982).

Smalley, Stephen, *John, Evangelist and Interpreter* (Greenwood: Attic, 1978).

Smith, D. Moody, *The Composition and Order of the Fourth Gospel. Bultmann's Literary Theory* (New Haven: Yale University, 1965).

————. *Johannine Christianity. Essays on Its Setting, Sources and Theology* (Columbia: University of South Carolina, 1984).

Stanley, David M., *"I Encountered God!" The Spiritual Exercises with the Gospel of St. John* (St. Louis: Institute of Jesuit Sources, 1986).

Staley, Jeffrey Lloyd, *The Print's First Kiss* (Atlanta: Scholars, 1988).

Teeple, Howard, *The Literary Origin of the Gospel of John* (Evanston: Religion and Ethics Institute, 1974).

Thompson, Marianne Meye, *The Humanity of Jesus in the Fourth Gospel* (Philadelphia: Fortress, 1988).

Thyen, Hartwig, "Aus der Literatur zum Johannesevangelium," *Theologische Rundschau* 39 (1974) and 42 (1977).

Von Wahlde, Urban C., *The Earliest Version of John's Gospel. Recovering the Gospel of Signs* (Wilmington: Michael Glazier, 1989).

————. *The Johannine Commandments. 1 John and the Struggle for the Johannine Tradition* (Mahwah: Paulist, 1990).

Vouga, François, "The Johannine School: A Gnostic Tradition in Primitive Christianity," *Biblica* 69 (1988), 371–85.

Wead, David W., *The Literary Devices in John's Gospel* (Basel: 1970).

White, M.C., *The Identity and Function of Jews and Related Terms in the Fourth Gospel* (Ann Arbor, microfilm, 1972).

Wijngaards, John, *The Gospel of John and His Letters* ("Message of Biblical Spirituality" 10; Wilmington: Michael Glazier, 1986).

Wilder, Amos N., *Theopoetic. Theology and the Religious Imagination* (Philadelphia: Westminster, 1976).

Wilkens, Wilhelm, *Die Entstehung des vierten Evangeliums* (Zollikon: Evangelischer, 1958).

Woll, Bruce, *Johannine Christianity in Conflict: Authority, Rank, and Succession in the First Farewell Discourse* (Chico: Scholars, 1981).

Yee, Gale A., *Jewish Feasts and the Gospel of John* (Wilmington: Michael Glazier, 1989).

Zorilla, Hugo C., *La fiesta de Liberación de los oprimidos* (University of Salamanca S.T.D. dissertation), summary in *Mission Focus* 13 (1985), 21–24.